P9-CCH-062

# V. I. LENIN

# TWO TACTICS OF
# SOCIAL-DEMOCRACY
# IN THE
# DEMOCRATIC REVOLUTION

FOREIGN LANGUAGES PRESS
PEKING 1970

First Edition    1965
Second Printing   1970

## PUBLISHER'S NOTE

The present English translation of V. I. Lenin's *Two Tactics of Social-Democracy in the Democratic Revolution* is a reprint of the text given in V. I. Lenin, *Selected Works*, English edition, Foreign Languages Publishing House, Moscow, 1952, Vol. I, Part 2. The notes at the end of the book are based on those given in the English edition and in the Chinese edition published by the People's Publishing House, Peking, in September 1964.

*Printed in the People's Republic of China*

# CONTENTS

# TWO TACTICS OF SOCIAL-DEMOCRACY IN THE DEMOCRATIC REVOLUTION[1]

## PREFACE

In a revolutionary period it is very difficult to keep abreast of events, which provide an astonishing amount of new material for an evaluation of the tactical slogans of revolutionary parties. The present pamphlet was written before the Odessa events.* We have already pointed out in the *Proletary*[2] (No. 9 — "Revolution Teaches")[3] that these events have forced even those Social-Democrats who created the "uprising-as-a-process" theory and who rejected propaganda for a provisional revolutionary government actually to pass over, or begin to pass over, to the side of their opponents. Revolution undoubtedly teaches with a rapidity and thoroughness which appear incredible in peaceful periods of political development. And, what is particularly important, it teaches not only the leaders, but the masses as well.

---

\* The reference is to the mutiny on the armoured cruiser *Potemkin.*[4] [Author's note to the 1907 edition.]

There is not the slightest doubt that the revolution will teach social-democratism to the masses of the workers in Russia. The revolution will confirm the program and tactics of Social-Democracy in actual practice, by demonstrating the true nature of the various classes of society, by demonstrating the bourgeois character of our democracy and the real aspirations of the peasantry, who, while being revolutionary in the bourgeois-democratic sense, harbour not the idea of "socialization," but of a new class struggle between the peasant bourgeoisie and the rural proletariat. The old illusions of the old Narodism, which are so clearly visible, for instance, in the draft program of the Socialist-Revolutionary Party on the question of the development of capitalism in Russia, the question of the democratic character of our "society" and the question of the significance of a complete victory of a peasant uprising — all these illusions will be mercilessly and completely blown to the winds by the revolution. For the first time it will give the various classes their real political baptism. These classes will emerge from the revolution with a definite political physiognomy, for they will have revealed themselves, not only in the programs and tactical slogans of their ideologists, but also in the open political action of the masses.

Undoubtedly, the revolution will teach us, and will teach the masses of the people. But the question that now confronts a militant political party is: shall we be able to teach the revolution anything? shall we be able to make use of the correctness of our Social-Democratic doctrine, of our bond with the only thoroughly revolutionary class, the proletariat, to put a proletarian imprint on the revolution, to carry the revolution to a real and decisive victory, not in word but in deed, and to paralyze the instability, halfheartedness and treachery of the democratic bourgeoisie?

It is to this end that we must direct all our efforts, and the achievement of it will depend, on the one hand, on the accuracy of our appraisal of the political situation, on the correctness of our tactical slogans, and, on the other hand, on whether these slogans will be backed by the real fighting strength of the masses of the workers. All the usual, regular, current work of all the organizations and groups of our Party, the work of propaganda, agitation and organization, is directed towards strengthening and expanding the ties with the masses. This work is always necessary; but in a revolutionary period less than in any other can it be considered sufficient. At such a time the working class feels an instinctive urge for open revolutionary action, and we must learn to set the aims of this action correctly, and then make these aims as widely known and understood as possible. It must not be forgotten that the current pessimism about our ties with the masses very often serves as a screen for bourgeois ideas regarding the role of the proletariat in the revolution. Undoubtedly, we still have a great deal to do to educate and organize the working class; but the whole question now is: where should the main political emphasis in this work of education and of organization be placed? On the trade unions and legally existing societies, or on armed insurrection, on the work of creating a revolutionary army and a revolutionary government? Both serve to educate and organize the working class. Both are, of course, necessary. But the whole question now, in the present revolution, amounts to this: what is to be emphasized in the work of educating and organizing the working class — the former or the latter?

The outcome of the revolution depends on whether the working class will play the part of a subsidiary to the bourgeoisie, a subsidiary that is powerful in the force of its onslaught against the autocracy but impotent politically, or whether it will play the part of leader of the people's revolution. The more intelligent representatives of the bourgeoisie are perfectly aware of this. That is precisely why the *Osvobozhdeniye*[5] praises Akimovism, Economism[6] in Social-Democracy, the trend, which is *now* placing the trade unions and the legally existing societies in the forefront. That is precisely why Mr. Struve welcomes (in the *Osvobozhdeniye*, No. 72) the Akimovist trends in the principles of the new *Iskra*. That is precisely why he comes down so heavily on the detested revolutionary narrowness of the decisions of the Third Congress of the Russian Social-Democratic Labour Party.

It is exceptionally important at the present time for Social-Democracy to have correct tactical slogans for leading the masses. There is nothing more dangerous in a revolutionary period than belittling the importance of tactical slogans that are sound in principle. For example, the *Iskra*,[7] in No. 104, actually passes over to the side of its opponents in the Social-Democratic movement, and yet, at the same time, disparages the importance of slogans and tactical decisions that are in front of the times and indicate the path along which the movement is proceeding, with a number of failures, errors, etc. On the contrary, the working out of correct tactical decisions is of immense importance for a party which, in the spirit of the sound principles of Marxism, desires to lead the proletariat and not merely to drag at the tail of events. In the resolutions of the Third Congress of the Russian Social-Democratic Labour Party and of the

Conference of the section which has seceded from the Party,* we have the most precise, most carefully thought-out, and most complete expression of tactical views — views not casually expressed by individual writers, but accepted by the responsible representatives of the Social-Democratic proletariat. Our Party is in advance of all the others, for it has a precise program, accepted by all. It must also set the other parties an example of strict adherence to its tactical resolutions, in contradistinction to the opportunism of the democratic bourgeoisie of the *Osvobozhdeniye* and the revolutionary phrasemongering of the Socialist-Revolutionaries, who only during the revolution suddenly thought of coming forward with a "draft" of a program and of investigating for the first time whether it is a bourgeois revolution that is going on in front of their eyes.

That is why we think it a most urgent task of the revolutionary Social-Democrats to study carefully the tactical resolutions of the Third Congress of the Russian Social-Democratic Labour Party and of the Conference, to define what deviations there are in them from the principles of Marxism, and to get a clear understanding of the concrete tasks of the Social-Democratic proletariat in a democratic revolution. It is to this task that the present pamphlet is devoted. The testing of our tactics from the standpoint of

---

* The Third Congress of the Russian Social-Democratic Labour Party (held in London in May 1905) was attended only by Bolsheviks, while in the "Conference" (held in Geneva at the same time) only Mensheviks participated. In the present pamphlet the latter are frequently referred to as "new *Iskra*-ists" because while continuing to publish the *Iskra* they declared, through their then adherent, Trotsky, that there was a gulf between the old and the new *Iskra*. [Author's note to the 1907 edition.]

the principles of Marxism and of the lessons of the revolution is also necessary for those who really desire to pave the way for unity of tactics as a basis for the future complete unity of the whole Russian Social-Democratic Labour Party, and not to confine themselves solely to verbal admonitions.

*N. Lenin*

July 1905

# 1. AN URGENT POLITICAL QUESTION

At the present revolutionary juncture the question of the convocation of a popular constituent assembly is on the order of the day. Opinions are divided on the point as to how this question should be settled. Three political trends are to be observed. The tsarist government admits the necessity of convening representatives of the people, but it does not want under any circumstances to permit their assembly to be a popular and a constituent assembly. It seems willing to agree, if we are to believe the newspaper reports on the work of the Bulygin Commission,[8] to an advisory assembly, to be elected without freedom to conduct agitation, and on the basis of restricted qualifications or a restricted class system. The revolutionary proletariat, inasmuch as it is led by the Social-Democratic Party, demands complete transfer of power to a constituent assembly, and for this purpose strives to obtain not only universal suffrage and complete freedom to conduct agitation, but also the immediate overthrow of the tsarist government and its replacement by a provisional revolutionary government. Finally, the liberal bourgeoisie, expressing its wishes through the leaders of the so-called "Constitutional-Democratic Party"[9] does not demand the overthrow of the tsarist government, does not advance the slogan of a provisional government and does not insist on real guarantees that the elections will be absolutely free and fair and that the assembly of representatives will be a genuinely popular and a genuinely constituent assembly. As a matter of fact, the liberal bourgeoisie, which is the only serious social support of the *Osvobozhdeniye* trend, is striving to effect as peaceful a deal as possible between the tsar and the revolutionary people, a deal, moreover, that would give a maximum of power to itself, the bourgeoisie, and a minimum to the revolutionary people — the proletariat and the peasantry.

Such is the political situation at the present time. Such are the three main political trends, corresponding to the three main social forces in contemporary Russia. We have already shown on more than one occasion (in the *Proletary*, Nos. 3, 4, 5)[10] how the *Osvobozhdentsi* use pseudodemocratic phrases to cover up their halfhearted, or, to put it more bluntly and plainly, their treacherous, perfidious policy towards the revolution. Let us now see how the Social-Democrats appraise the tasks of the moment. Excellent material for this purpose is provided by the two resolutions that were passed quite recently by the Third Congress of the Russian Social-Democratic Labour Party and by the "Conference" of the section which has seceded from the Party. The question as to which of these resolutions more correctly appraises the political situation and more correctly defines the tactics of the revolutionary proletariat is of enormous importance, and every Social-Democrat who is anxious to fulfil his duties as a propagandist, agitator and organizer intelligently, must study this question with the closest attention, leaving all irrelevant considerations entirely aside.

By the Party's tactics we mean the Party's political conduct, or the character, the direction and methods of its
political activity. Tactical resolutions are adopted by Party
congresses in order precisely to define the political conduct
of the Party as a whole with regard to new tasks, or in view
of a new political situation. Such a new situation has been
created by the revolution that has started in Russia, i.e., the
complete, resolute and open rupture between the over-
whelming majority of the people and the tsarist government.
The new question concerns the practical methods to be
adopted in convening a genuinely popular and genuinely constituent assembly (the theoretical question concerning such
an assembly was officially settled by Social-Democracy long
ago, before all other parties, in its Party program). Since the
people have broken with the government, and the masses
realize the necessity of setting up a new order, the party
which set itself the object of overthrowing the government
must necessarily consider what government to put up in place
of the old, deposed government. A *new* question concerning
a provisional revolutionary government arises. In order to
give a complete answer to this question the Party of the
class-conscious proletariat must make clear: 1) the *significance* of a provisional revolutionary government in the revolution that is now going on and in the entire struggle of
the proletariat in general; 2) its *attitude* towards a provisional revolutionary government; 3) the precise conditions of
Social-Democratic *participation* in this government; 4) the
conditions under which pressure is to be brought to bear on
this government from *below*, i.e., in the event of there being
no Social-Democrats in it. Only after all these questions are
made clear, will the political conduct of the Party in this
sphere be principled, clear and firm.

9

Let us now consider how the resolution of the Third Congress of the Russian Social-Democratic Labour Party answers these questions. The following is the full text of the resolution:

*"Resolution on a Provisional Revolutionary Government*
"Whereas:

"1) both the immediate interests of the proletariat and the interests of its struggle for the final aims of Socialism require the fullest possible measure of political liberty and, consequently, the replacement of the autocratic form of government by a democratic republic;

"2) the establishment of a democratic republic in Russia is possible only as a result of a victorious popular insurrection whose organ will be a provisional revolutionary government, which alone will be capable of ensuring complete freedom of agitation during the election campaign and of convening a constituent assembly that will really express the will of the people, an assembly elected on the basis of universal and equal suffrage, direct elections and secret ballot;

"3) under the present social and economic order this democratic revolution in Russia will not weaken, but strengthen the rule of the bourgeoisie, which at a certain moment will inevitably try, stopping at nothing, to take away from the Russian proletariat as many of the gains of the revolutionary period as possible:

"The Third Congress of the Russian Social-Democratic Labour Party resolves that:

"a) it is necessary to disseminate among the working class a concrete idea of the most probable course of the revolution and of the necessity, at a certain moment in the revolution, for the appearance of a provisional revolutionary government, from which the proletariat will demand the realization of all the immediate political and economic demands contained in our program (the minimum program);

"b)  subject to the relation of forces, and other factors which cannot be exactly determined beforehand, representatives of our Party may participate in the provisional revolutionary government for the purpose of relentless struggle against all counterrevolutionary attempts and of the defence of the independent interests of the working class;

"c)  an indispensable condition for such participation is that the Party should exercise strict control over its representatives and that the independence of the Social-Democratic Party, which is striving for a complete socialist revolution and, consequently, is irreconcilably hostile to all bourgeois parties, should be strictly maintained;

"d)  irrespective whether the participation of Social-Democrats in the provisional revolutionary government prove possible or not, we must propagate among the broadest masses of the proletariat the necessity for permanent pressure to be brought to bear upon the provisional government by the armed proletariat, led by the Social-Democratic Party, for the purpose of defending, consolidating and extending the gains of the revolution."

## 2. WHAT DOES THE RESOLUTION OF THE THIRD CONGRESS OF THE R.S.D.L.P. ON A PROVISIONAL REVOLUTIONARY GOVERNMENT TEACH US?

The resolution of the Third Congress of the Russian Social-Democratic Labour Party, as is evident from its title, is devoted wholly and exclusively to the question of a provisional revolutionary government. Hence, the question as to whether Social-Democrats may participate in a provisional revolutionary government is included in it as part of the whole question. On the other hand, it deals only with a provisional revolutionary government and with nothing else; consequently, it completely leaves out, for example, the question of the "conquest of power" in general, etc. Was the Congress right in eliminating this and similar questions? Undoubtedly it was right, because the political situation in Russia does not at all give rise to such questions as immediate issues. On the contrary, the issue raised by the whole of the people at the present time is the overthrow of the autocracy and the convocation of a constituent assembly. Party congresses should take up and decide not issues which this or that writer happened to touch upon opportunely or inopportunely, but such as are of vital political importance by reason of the prevailing conditions and the objective course of social development.

Of what importance is a provisional revolutionary government in the present revolution, and in the general struggle of the proletariat? The resolution of the Congress explains this by pointing at the very outset to the need for the "fullest possible measure of political liberty," both from the standpoint of the immediate interests of the proletariat and from the standpoint of the "final aims of Socialism." And complete political liberty requires that the tsarist autocracy be replaced by a democratic republic, as our Party program has already recognized. The stress laid in the Congress resolution on the slogan of a democratic republic is necessary both as a matter of logic and in point of principle, for it is precisely complete freedom that the proletariat, as the foremost champion of democracy, is striving to attain. Moreover, it is all the more advisable to stress this at the present time because right now the monarchists, namely, the so-called constitutional-"democratic" party, or party of "liberation," in our country, are flying the flag of "democracy." In order to establish a republic it is absolutely necessary to have an assembly of people's representatives; and it must be a popular (elected on the basis of universal and equal suffrage, direct elections and secret ballot), and a constituent assembly. This too is recognized in the Congress resolution, further on. But the resolution does not stop there. In order to establish the new order "that will really express the will of the people" it is not enough to call a representative assembly a constituent assembly. This assembly must have the authority and power to "constitute." Taking this into consideration, the resolution of the Congress does not confine itself to the formal slogan of a "constituent assembly," but adds the material conditions which alone will enable that assembly really to carry out its tasks. Such specification of the conditions that will enable an assembly which is constituent in name to become constituent in fact is imperatively necessary, for, as we have pointed out more than once, the liberal bourgeoisie, as represented by the Constitutional-Monarchist Party, is deliberately distorting the slogan of a popular constituent assembly and reducing it to a hollow phrase.

The Congress resolution states that a provisional revolutionary government *alone*, one, moreover, that will be the organ of a victorious popular insurrection, can secure full freedom of agitation in the election campaign and convene an assembly that will really express the will of the people. Is this postulate correct? Whoever took it into his head to dispute it would have to assert that it is possible for the tsarist government not to side with the reaction, that it is capable of being neutral during the elections, that it will see to it that the will of the people is really expressed. Such assertions are so absurd that no one would venture to defend them openly; but they are being surreptitiously smuggled in under liberal colours, by our liberationists. Somebody must convene the constituent assembly, somebody must guarantee the freedom and fairness of the elections; somebody must invest such an assembly with full power and authority. Only a revolutionary government, which is the organ of the insurrection, can desire this in all sincerity and be capable of doing all that is required to achieve this. The tsarist government will inevitably counteract this. A liberal government, which will come to terms with the tsar, and which does not rely entirely on the popular uprising, cannot sincerely desire this, and could not accomplish it even if it most sincerely desired to. Therefore, the resolution of the Congress gives the only correct and entirely consistent democratic slogan.

But an evaluation of the significance of a provisional revolutionary government would be incomplete and false if the class nature of the democratic revolution were lost sight of. The resolution therefore adds that the revolution will strengthen the rule of the bourgeoisie. This is inevitable under the present, i.e., capitalist, social and economic system. And the strengthening of the rule of the bourgeoisie over the proletariat which has secured some measure of political liberty must inevitably lead to a desperate struggle between them for power, must lead to desperate attempts on the part of the bourgeoisie "to take away from the proletariat the gains of the revolutionary period." Therefore the proletariat, which is fighting for democracy in front of all and at the head of all, must not for a single moment forget about the new antagonisms that are inherent in bourgeois democracy and about the new struggle.

Thus, the section of the resolution which we have just reviewed fully appraises the significance of a provisional revolutionary government in its relation to the struggle for freedom and for a republic, in its relation to a constituent assembly and in its relation to the democratic revolution, which clears the ground for a new class struggle.

The next question is what should be the attitude of the proletariat in general towards a provisional revolutionary government? The Congress resolution answers this first of all by directly advising the Party to spread among the working class the conviction that a provisional revolutionary government is necessary. The working class must be made aware of this necessity. Whereas the "democratic" bourgeoisie leaves the question of overthrowing the tsarist government in the shade, we must push it to the fore and insist on the need for a provisional revolutionary government. More than that, we must outline for such a government a program of action that will conform with the objective conditions of the historic period through which we are now passing and with the aims of proletarian democracy. This program is the *entire* minimum program of our Party, the program of the immediate political and economic reforms which, on the one hand, can be fully realized on the basis of the existing social and economic relationships and, on the other hand, are requisite for the next step forward, for the achievement of Socialism.

Thus, the resolution fully elucidates the nature and aims of a provisional revolutionary government. By its origin and fundamental nature such a government must be the organ of the popular insurrection. Its formal purpose must be to serve as the instrument for convening a popular constituent assembly. The substance of its activities must be to put into effect the minimum program of proletarian democracy, the only program capable of safeguarding the interests of the people which has risen against the autocracy.

It might be argued that being only provisional, a provisional government cannot carry out a constructive program which has not yet received the approval of the entire people. Such an argument would merely be the sophistry of reactionaries and "absolutists." To abstain from carrying out a constructive program means tolerating the existence of the feudal regime of the putrid autocracy. Such a regime could be tolerated only by a government of traitors to the cause of the revolution, but not by a government which is the organ of a popular insurrection. It would be mockery for anyone to propose that we should refrain from exercising freedom of assembly pending the confirmation of such freedom by a constituent assembly, on the plea that the constituent assembly might not confirm freedom of assembly! It is equal mockery to object to the immediate execution of the minimum program by a provisional revolutionary government.

Finally, we will note that by making it the task of the provisional revolutionary government to put into effect the minimum program, the resolution eliminated the absurd, semianarchist ideas about putting the maximum program into effect immediately, about the conquest of power for a socialist revolution. The degree of economic development of Russia (an objective condition) and the degree of class consciousness and organization of the broad masses of the proletariat (a subjective condition inseparably connected with the objective condition) make the immediate complete emancipation of the working class impossible. Only the most ignorant people can ignore the bourgeois nature of the democratic revolution which is now taking place; only the most naive optimists can forget how little as yet the masses of the workers are informed about the aims of Socialism and about the methods of achieving it. And we are all convinced that the emancipation of the workers can be effected only by the workers themselves; a socialist revolution is out of the question unless the masses become class conscious and organized, trained and educated in open class struggle against the entire bourgeoisie. In answer to the anarchist objections that we are putting off the socialist revolution, we say: we are not putting it off, but we are taking the first step towards it in the only possible way, along the only correct road, namely, the road of a democratic republic. Whoever wants to reach Socialism by a different road, other than that of political democracy, will inevitably arrive at conclusions that are absurd and reactionary both in the economic and the political sense. If any workers ask us at the given moment why we should not go ahead and carry out our maximum program, we shall answer by pointing out how far the masses of the democratically-minded people still are from Socialism, how undeveloped class antagonisms still are, how unorganized the proletarians still are. Organize hundreds of thousands of workers all over Russia; enlist the sympathy of millions for our program! Try to do this without confining yourselves to high-sounding but hollow anarchist phrases — and you will see at once that in order to achieve this organization, in order to spread this socialist enlightenment, we must achieve the fullest possible measure of democratic reforms.

Let us proceed further. Once we are clear about the importance of a provisional revolutionary government and the attitude of the proletariat toward it, the following question arises: is it permissible for us to participate in it (action from above) and, if so, under what conditions? What should be our action from below? The resolution supplies precise answers to both these questions. It emphatically declares that it is *permissible* in principle for Social-Democrats to participate in a provisional revolutionary government (during the period of a democratic revolution, the period of struggle for a republic). By this declaration we once and for all dissociate ourselves both from the anarchists, who answer this question in the negative on principle, and from the *khvostists* among the Social-Democrats (like Martynov and the new *Iskra*-ists) who have *tried to frighten* us with the prospect of a situation wherein it might prove necessary for us to participate in such a government. By this declaration the Third Congress of the Russian Social-Democratic Labour Party rejected, once and for all, the idea expressed by the new *Iskra* that the participation of Social-Democrats in a provisional revolutionary government would be a variety of Millerandism,[11] that it is impermissible in principle, as sanctifying the bourgeois order, etc.

But permissibility in principle does not, of course, solve the question of practical expediency. Under what conditions is this new form of struggle — the struggle "from above" recognized by the Party Congress — expedient? It goes without saying that at the present time it is impossible to speak of concrete conditions, such as relation of forces, etc., and the resolution, naturally, refrains from defining these conditions in advance. No intelligent person would venture at the present time to prophesy anything on this subject. What we can and must do is determine the nature and aim of our participation. This is precisely what is done in the resolution, which points out two objectives of our participation: 1) a relentless struggle against counterrevolutionary attempts, and 2) the defence of the independent interests of the working class. At a time when the liberal bourgeoisie is beginning to talk assiduously about the psychology of reaction (see Mr. Struve's most instructive "Open Letter" in the *Osvobozhdeniye*, No. 71) in an attempt to frighten the revolutionary people and induce it to show compliance towards the autocracy — at such a time it is particularly appropriate for the party of the proletariat to call attention to the task of waging a real war against counterrevolution. In the final analysis, force alone settles the great problems of political liberty and the class struggle, and it is our business to prepare and organize this force and to employ it actively, not only for defence, but also for attack. The long reign of political reaction in Europe, which has lasted almost uninterruptedly since the days of the Paris Commune, has too greatly accustomed us to the idea that action can proceed only "from below," has too greatly inured us to seeing only defensive struggles. We have now, undoubtedly, entered a new era: a period of political upheavals and revolutions has begun. In a period such as Russia is passing through at the present time, it is impermissible to confine ourselves to old, stereotyped formulae. We must propagate the idea of action from above, we must prepare for the most energetic, offensive action, and must study the conditions for and forms of such actions. The Congress resolution puts two of these conditions into the forefront: one refers to the formal aspect of Social-Democratic participation in a provisional revolutionary government (strict control by the Party over its representatives), the other to the very nature of such participation (never for an instant to lose sight of the aim of effecting a complete socialist revolution).

Having thus explained from all aspects the Party's policy with regard to action "from above" — this new, hitherto almost unprecedented method of struggle — the resolution also provides for the eventuality that we shall not be able to act from above. We must exercise pressure on the provisional revolutionary government from below in any case. In order to be able to exercise this pressure from below, the proletariat must be armed — for in a revolutionary situation matters develop with exceptional rapidity to the stage of open civil war — and must be led by the Social-Democratic Party. The object of its armed pressure is that of "defending, consolidating and extending the gains of the revolution," i.e., those gains which from the standpoint of the interests of the proletariat must consist in the fulfilment of the whole of our minimum program.

With this we conclude our brief analysis of the resolution of the Third Congress on a provisional revolutionary government. As the reader can see, the resolution explains the importance of this new question, the attitude of the Party of the proletariat toward it, and the policy the Party must pursue both inside a provisional revolutionary government and outside of it.

Let us now consider the corresponding resolution of the "Conference."

# 3. WHAT IS A "DECISIVE VICTORY OF THE REVOLUTION OVER TSARISM"?

The resolution of the "Conference" is devoted to the question: *"The conquest of power and participation in a provisional government."** As we have already pointed out, the very manner in which the question is presented betrays confusion. On the one hand, the question is presented in a narrow way: it deals only with our participation in a provisional government and not with the Party's tasks in regard to a provisional revolutionary government in general. On the other hand, two totally different questions are confused, viz., the question of our participation at one of the stages of the *democratic* revolution, and the question of the *socialist* revolution. Indeed, the "conquest of power" by Social-Democracy is a socialist revolution, nor can it be anything else if we use these words in their direct and usually accepted sense. If, however, we are to understand these words to mean the conquest of power for a democratic revolution and not for a socialist revolution, then what is the point in talking not only about participation in a provisional revolutionary government but also about the "conquest of power" *in general*? Obviously our "Conferencers" were not very clear themselves as to what they should talk about: the democratic or the socialist revolution. Those who have followed the literature on this question know that it was Comrade Martynov, in his notorious *Two Dictatorships*, who started

---

* The full text of this resolution can be reconstructed by the reader from the quotations given on pp. 400, 403, 407, 431 and 433 of this pamphlet. [Author's note to the 1907 edition. See in this book pp. 22, 29-30, 36-37, 80, 85-86 — *Ed.*]

this muddle: the new *Iskra*-ists are reluctant to recall the manner in which this question was presented (before January 9)[12] in that model of a *khvostist* work. Nevertheless, there can be no doubt that it exercised ideological influence on the Conference.

But let us leave the title of the resolution. Its contents reveal mistakes incomparably more profound and serious. Here is the first part:

"A decisive victory of the revolution over tsarism may be marked either by the establishment of a provisional government, which will emerge from a victorious popular insurrection, or by the revolutionary initiative of a representative institution of one kind or another, which, under direct revolutionary pressure of the people, decides to set up a popular constituent assembly."

Thus, we are told that a decisive victory of the revolution over tsarism may be marked either by a victorious insurrection, or . . . by a decision of a representative institution to set up a constituent assembly! What does this mean? How are we to understand it? A decisive victory may be marked by a "decision" to set up a constituent assembly?? And such a "victory" is put side by side with the establishment of a provisional government which will "emerge from a victorious popular insurrection"!! The Conference failed to note that a *victorious* popular insurrection and the *establishment* of a provisional government would signify the victory of the revolution *in actual fact*, whereas a "decision" to set up a constituent assembly would signify a victory of the revolution *in words* only.

The Conference of the Mensheviks, or new *Iskra*-ists, committed the same error that the liberals, the *Osvobozh-*

*dentsi* are constantly committing. The *Osvobozhdentsi* prattle about a "constituent" assembly and bashfully shut their eyes to the fact that power and authority remain in the hands of the tsar, forgetting that in order to "constitute" one must possess the *power* to do so. The Conference also forgot that it is a far cry from a "decision" adopted by representatives — no matter who they are — to the fulfilment of that decision. The Conference further forgot that so long as power remained in the hands of the tsar, all decisions passed by any representatives whatsoever would remain empty and miserable prattle, as was the case with the "decisions" of the Frankfurt Parliament, famous in the history of the German Revolution of 1848. In his *Neue Rheinische Zeitung*,[13] Marx, the representative of the revolutionary proletariat, castigated the Frankfurt liberal *Osvobozhdentsi* with merciless sarcasm precisely because they uttered fine words, adopted all sorts of democratic "decisions," "constituted" all kinds of liberties, while actually they left power in the hands of the king and failed to organize an armed struggle against the military forces at the disposal of the king. And while the Frankfurt *Osvobozhdentsi* were prattling — the king bided his time, consolidated his military forces, and the counterrevolution, relying on real force, utterly routed the democrats with all their fine "decisions."

The Conference put on a par with a decisive victory the very thing that lacks the essential condition of victory. How was it possible for Social-Democrats who recognize the republican program of our Party to commit such an error? In order to understand this strange phenomenon we must turn to the resolution of the Third Congress on the section which has seceded from the Party.* This resolution refers to the fact that various trends "akin to Economism" have survived in our Party. Our "Conferencers" (it is not for nothing that they are under the ideological guidance of Martynov) talk of the revolution in exactly the same way as the Economists talked of the political struggle or the eight-hour day. The Economists immediately gave currency to the "theory of stages": 1) the struggle for rights, 2) political agitation, 3) political struggle; or, 1) a ten-hour day, 2) a nine-hour day, 3) an eight-hour day. The results of this

---

* We cite this resolution in full. "The Congress places on record that since the time of the Party's fight against Economism, certain trends have survived in the R.S.D.L.P. which, in various degrees and respects, are akin to Economism and which betray a common tendency to belittle the importance of the elements of consciousness in the proletarian struggle, and to subordinate it to the element of spontaneity. On questions of organization, the representatives of these trends put forward, in theory, the organization-as-a-process principle, which is out of harmony with methodical Party work, while in practice they systematically deviate from Party discipline in very many cases, and in other cases preach to the least enlightened section of the Party the idea of a wide application of the elective principle, without taking into consideration the objective conditions of Russian life, and so strive to undermine the only basis for Party ties that is possible at the present time. In tactical questions they betray a striving to narrow the scope of Party work, declaring their opposition to the Party pursuing completely independent tactics in relation to the liberal-bourgeois parties, denying that it is possible and desirable for our Party to assume the role of organizer in the people's insurrection and opposing the participation of the Party in a provisional democratic-revolutionary government under any conditions whatsoever.

"The Congress instructs all Party members everywhere to conduct an energetic ideological struggle against such partial deviations from the principles of revolutionary Social-Democracy; at the same time, however, it is of the opinion that persons who share such views to any degree may belong to Party organizations on the indispensable condition that they recognize the Party congresses and the Party Rules and wholly submit to Party discipline." [Author's note to the 1907 edition.]

"tactics-as-a-process" are sufficiently well known to all. Now we are invited nicely to divide the revolution too in advance into the following stages: 1) the tsar convenes a representative body; 2) this representative body "decides" under pressure of the "people" to set up a constituent assembly; 3) . . . the Mensheviks have not yet agreed among themselves as to the third stage; they have forgotten that the revolutionary pressure of the people will meet with the counterrevolutionary pressure of tsarism and that, therefore, either the "decision" will remain unfulfilled or the issue will be decided after all by the victory or the defeat of the popular insurrection. The resolution of the Conference is an exact reproduction of the following reasoning of the Economists: a decisive victory of the workers may be marked either by the realization of the eight-hour day in a revolutionary way, or by the grant of a ten-hour day and a "decision" to go over to a nine-hour day. . . . Exactly the same.

It may be objected, perhaps, that the authors of the resolution did not mean *to place* the victory of an insurrection *on a par* with the "decision" of a representative institution convened by the tsar, that they only wanted to provide for the Party's tactics in either case. To this our answer would be: 1) The text of the resolution plainly and unambiguously describes the *decision* of a representative institution as "a decisive victory of the revolution over tsarism." Perhaps that is the result of careless wording, perhaps it could be corrected after consulting the minutes, but, so long as it is not corrected, the present wording can have only one meaning, and this meaning is entirely in keeping with the *Osvobozhdeniye* line of reasoning. 2) The *Osvobozhdeniye* line of reasoning, into which the authors of the resolution have drifted,

25

stands out in incomparably greater relief in other literary productions of the new *Iskra*-ists. For instance, the organ of the Tiflis Committee, *Sotsial-Demokrat*[14] (in the Georgian language; praised by the *Iskra* in No. 100), in the article "The Zemsky Sobor and Our Tactics," goes so far as to say that the "tactics" "which make the Zemsky Sobor the centre of our activities" (about the convocation of which, we may add, nothing definite is known as yet!) *"are more advantageous for us"* than the "tactics" of armed insurrection and the establishment of a provisional revolutionary government. We shall refer to this article again further on. 3) No objection can be made to a preliminary discussion of what tactics the Party should adopt in the event of the victory of the revolution as well as in the event of its defeat, in the event of a successful insurrection as well as in the event of the insurrection failing to develop into a serious force. It is possible that the tsarist government will succeed in convening a representative assembly for the purpose of coming to terms with the liberal bourgeoisie; providing for that eventuality, the resolution of the Third Congress speaks plainly about "hypocritical policy," "pseudo democracy," "a travesty of popular representation, something like the so-called Zemsky Sobor."* But the whole point is that this

---

* The following is the text of this resolution on the attitude towards the tactics of the government on the eve of the revolution:

"Whereas for purposes of self-preservation the government during the present revolutionary period, while intensifying the usual measures of repression directed mainly against the class-conscious elements of the proletariat, at the same time 1) tries by means of concessions and promises of reform to corrupt the working class politically and thereby to divert it from the revolutionary struggle; 2) with the same object clothes its hypocritical policy of concessions in pseudodemocratic forms, beginning with an invitation to the workers to elect their representatives to comis not said in the resolution on a provisional revolutionary government, for it has nothing to do with a provisional revolutionary government. This eventuality defers the problem of the insurrection and of the establishment of a provisional revolutionary government; it alters this problem, etc. The point in question now is not that all kinds of combinations are possible, that both victory and defeat are possible, that there may be direct or circuitous paths; the point is that it is impermissible for a Social-Democrat to cause confusion in the minds of the workers concerning the genuinely revolutionary path, that it is impermissible, to describe in the *Osvobozhdeniye* manner, as a decisive victory that which lacks the *main* requisite for victory. It is possible that even

---

missions and conferences and ending with the establishment of a travesty of popular representation, something like the so-called Zemsky Sobor; 3) organizes the so-called Black Hundreds and incites against the revolution all those elements of the people in general who are reactionary, ignorant or blinded by racial or religious hatred:

"The Third Congress of the R.S.D.L.P. resolves to call on all Party organizations:

"a) while exposing the reactionary purpose of the government's concessions, to emphasize in their propaganda and agitation the fact that, on the one hand, these concessions were granted under compulsion, and, on the other, that it is absolutely impossible for the autocracy to grant reforms satisfactory to the proletariat;

"b) taking advantage of the election campaign, to explain to the workers the real significance of the government's measures and to show that it is necessary for the proletariat to convene by revolutionary means a constituent assembly on the basis of universal and equal suffrage, direct elections and secret ballot;

"c) to organize the proletariat for the immediate realization, in a revolutionary way, of the eight-hour working day and of the other immediate demands of the working class;

"d) to organize armed resistance to the actions of the Black Hundreds, and generally, of all reactionary elements led by the government." [Author's note to the 1907 edition.]

the eight-hour day we will get not at one stroke, but only by a long and roundabout way; but what would you say of a man who calls such impotence, such weakness as renders the proletariat *incapable* of counteracting procrastination, delays, haggling, treachery and reaction, a victory for the workers? It is possible that the Russian revolution will end in an "abortive constitution," as was once stated in the *Vperyod,*\* but can this justify a Social-Democrat, who on the eve of a decisive struggle would call this abortion a "decisive victory over tsarism"? It is possible that, at the worst, not only will we not win a republic, but that even the constitution we will get will be an illusory one, a constitution "à la Shipov,"[15] but would it be pardonable for a Social-Democrat to obscure our slogan of a republic?

Of course the new *Iskra*-ists have not as yet gone so far as to obscure it. But the degree to which the revolutionary spirit has fled from them, the degree to which lifeless pedantry has blinded them to the militant tasks of the moment is most vividly shown by the fact that in their resolution they, of all things, *forgot* to say a word about the republic. It is incredible, but it is a fact. All the slogans of Social-Democracy were endorsed, repeated, explained and presented in detail in the various resolutions of the Conference — even the election of shop stewards and deputies by the workers

---

\* The newspaper *Vperyod*, published in Geneva, began to appear in January 1905 as the organ of the Bolshevik section of the Party. From January to May, eighteen issues appeared. After May, by virtue of the decision of the Third Congress of the Russian Social-Democratic Labour Party, the *Proletary* was issued in place of the *Vperyod* as the central organ of the R.S.D.L.P. (This Congress took place in May, in London; the Mensheviks did not appear; they organized their own "Conference" in Geneva.) [Author's note to the 1907 edition.]

was not forgotten, but in a resolution on a provisional revolutionary government they simply did not find occasion to mention the republic. To talk of the "victory" of the people's insurrection, of the establishment of a provisional government, and not to indicate what relation these "steps" and acts have to the winning of a republic — means writing a resolution not for the guidance of the proletarian struggle, but for the purpose of hobbling along at the tail end of the proletarian movement.

To sum up: the first part of the resolution 1) gave no explanation whatever of the significance of a provisional revolutionary government from the standpoint of the struggle for a republic and of securing a genuinely popular and genuinely constituent assembly; 2) confused the democratic consciousness of the proletariat by placing on a par with a decisive victory of the revolution over tsarism a state of affairs in which precisely the main requisite for a real victory is lacking.

## 4. THE ABOLITION OF THE MONARCHIST SYSTEM AND THE REPUBLIC

Let us pass on to the next section of the resolution:
". . . in either case such a victory will inaugurate a new phase in the revolutionary epoch.

"The task which the objective conditions of social development spontaneously raise in this new phase is the final abolition of the whole regime of social estates and of the monarchy in the process of mutual struggle among the elements of politically emancipated bourgeois society for the satisfaction of their social interests and for the direct acquisition of power.

"Therefore, the provisional government that would undertake to carry out the tasks of this revolution, which by its historical nature is a bourgeois revolution, would also, in regulating the mutual struggle of the antagonistic classes within the nation in the process of emancipation, not only have to push revolutionary development further forward but also fight against those of its factors which threaten the foundation of the capitalist system."

Let us examine this section which forms an independent part of the resolution. The idea underlying the above-quoted arguments coincides with that stated in the third clause of the Congress resolution. But in comparing these parts of the two resolutions, the following radical difference at once becomes apparent. The Congress resolution, describing in a few words the social and economic basis of the revolution, concentrates attention entirely on the sharply defined struggle of classes for definite gains and places the militant tasks of the proletariat in the forefront. The resolution of the Conference, in a long, nebulous and confused description of the social and economic basis of the revolution, speaks very vaguely about a struggle for definite gains and leaves the militant tasks of the proletariat altogether in the shade. The resolution of the Conference speaks of the abolition of the old order in the process of mutual struggle among the various elements of society. The Congress resolution says that we, the Party of the proletariat, must effect this abolition, that only the establishment of a democratic republic signifies the real abolition of the old order, that we must win such a republic, that we shall fight for it and for complete liberty, not only against the autocracy, but also against the bourgeoisie, when it attempts (for it will surely attempt) to wrest our gains from us. The Congress resolution calls on a definite class to wage a struggle for a precisely defined immediate aim. The resolution of the Conference discourses on the mutual struggle of various forces. One resolution expresses the psychology of active struggle, the other expresses that of the passive onlooker; one resounds with the call for live action, the other is steeped in lifeless pedantry. Both resolutions state that the present revolution is only our first step, which will be followed by a second; but from this, one resolution draws the conclusion that we must all the more quickly make this first step, all the more quickly get it over, win a republic, mercilessly crush the counter-revolution and prepare the ground for the second step. The other resolution, however, oozes, so to speak, with verbose descriptions of the first step and (excuse the vulgar expression) chews the cud over it. The resolution of the Congress takes the old and eternally new ideas of Marxism (about the bourgeois nature of a democratic revolution) as a preface or first premise from which it draws conclusions as to the progressive tasks of the advanced class, which is fighting both for the democratic and for the socialist revolution. The resolution of the Conference does not go beyond the preface, chewing it over and over again and trying to be clever about it.

This is the very distinction which has long divided the Russian Marxists into two wings: the moralizing and the militant wings of the old days of "legal Marxism," and the economic and political wings of the period of the nascent mass movement. From the correct premise of Marxism concerning the deep economic roots of the class struggle in general and of the political struggle in particular, the Economists drew the singular conclusion that we must turn our backs on the political struggle and retard its development, narrow its scope and reduce its aims. The political wing, on the contrary, drew a different conclusion from these same premises, namely, that the deeper the roots of our struggle at the present time, the more widely, the more boldly, the more resolutely and with greater initiative must we wage this struggle. We have the very same controversy before us now, only under different circumstances and in a different form. From the premises that a democratic revolution is far from being a socialist one, that the propertyless are not by any means the only ones to be "interested" in it, that it is deeply rooted in the inexorable needs and requirements of the *whole* of bourgeois society — from these premises we draw the conclusion that the advanced class must formulate its democratic aims all the more boldly, express them all the more sharply and completely, put forward the direct slogan of a republic, popularize the idea that a provisional revolutionary government is needed and that it is necessary ruthlessly to crush the counterrevolution. Our opponents, the new *Iskra*-ists, however, deduce from these very same premises that the democratic conclusions should not be expressed fully, that the slogan of a republic may be omitted from the practical slogans, that we can refrain from popularizing the idea that a provisional revolutionary government is needed, that a mere decision to convene a constituent assembly can be termed a decisive victory, that we need not advance the task of combating counterrevolution as our active aim but that we may submerge it in a nebulous (and, as we shall presently see, wrongly formulated) reference to a "process of mutual struggle." This is not the language of political leaders, but of archive mummies.

And the more closely one examines the various formulae in the new *Iskra*-ist resolution, the clearer its aforementioned basic features become. We are told, for instance, of a "process of mutual struggle among the elements of politically emancipated bourgeois society." Bearing in mind the subject with which this resolution deals (a provisional revolutionary government) one asks in astonishment: if you are referring to the process of mutual struggle, how can you keep silent about the elements which are politically *enslaving* bourgeois society? Do the "Conferencers" really imagine that because they have assumed that the revolution will be victorious these elements have already disappeared? Such an idea would be absurd in general, and would be an expression of the greatest political naïveté and political shortsightedness in particular. After the victory of the revolution over the counterrevolution, the latter will not disappear; on the contrary, it will inevitably start a new and even more desperate struggle. Since the purpose of our resolution is to analyze the tasks that will confront us when the revolution is victorious, it is our duty to devote enormous attention to the tasks of repelling counterrevolutionary attacks (as is done in the resolution of the Congress), and not submerge these immediate, urgent and vital political tasks of a militant party in general discussions on what will happen *after* the present revolutionary period, what will happen when a "politically *emancipated* society" will already be in existence. Just as the Economists, by repeating the general truism that politics are subordinated to economics, covered up their failure to understand current political tasks, so the new *Iskra*-ists, by repeating the general truism that struggles will take place in a politically *emancipated* society, cover up their failure to understand the urgent revolutionary tasks of the political *emancipation* of this society.

Take the expression "the final abolition of the whole regime of social estates and the monarchy." In plain language, the final abolition of the monarchist system means the establishment of a democratic republic. But our good Martynov and his admirers think that this expression is far too simple and clear. They insist on rendering it "more profound" and saying it more "cleverly." As a result, we get, on the one hand, ridiculous and vain efforts to appear profound; on the other hand, we get a description instead of a slogan, a sort of melancholy looking backward instead of a stirring appeal to march forward. We get the impression, not of living people eager to fight for a republic here and now, but of fossilized mummies who *sub specie aeternitatis*[16] consider the question from the standpoint of *plusquamperfectum.*[17]

Let us proceed further: ". . . the provisional government . . . would undertake to carry out the tasks of this . . . bourgeois revolution." . . . Here we see at once the result of the fact that our "Conferencers" have overlooked a concrete question which confronts the political leaders of the proletariat. The concrete question of a provisional revolutionary government was obscured from their field of vision by the question of the future series of governments which will carry out the aims of the bourgeois revolution in general. If you want to consider the question "historically," the example of any European country will show you that it was a series of governments, not by any means "provisional," that carried out the historical aims of the bourgeois revolution, that even the governments which defeated the revolution were nonetheless forced to carry out the historical aims of that defeated revolution. But what is called a "provisional revolutionary government" is something altogether different from what you are referring to: that is the name given to the government of a revolutionary epoch, which directly replaces the overthrown government and rests on the insurrection of the people, and not on some kind of representative institutions coming from the people. A provisional revolutionary government is the organ of struggle for the immediate victory of the revolution, for immediately repelling counterrevolutionary attempts, and not by any means an organ for carrying out the historical aims of the bourgeois revolution in general. Gentlemen, let us leave it to the future historians of a future *Russkaya Starina*[18] to determine exactly what aims of the bourgeois revolution we, or this or that government, shall have achieved — there will be time enough to do that thirty years from now; at present we must put forward slogans and give practical directives for the struggle for a republic and for the proletariat's most active participation in this struggle.

For the reasons stated, the last propositions in the section of the resolution which we have quoted above are also unsatisfactory. The expression that the provisional government would have to "regulate" the mutual struggle among the antagonistic classes is exceedingly inapt, or at any rate awkwardly put; Marxists should not use such liberal, *Osvobozhdeniye* formulations, which lead one to believe that it is possible to have governments which serve not as organs of the class struggle but as its "regulators". . . . The government would "not only have to push revolutionary development further forward but also fight against those of its factors which threaten the foundations of the capitalist system." But it is the proletariat, the very same in whose name the resolution is speaking, that constitutes this "factor"! Instead of indicating just how the proletariat should "push revolutionary development further forward" at the present time (push it further than the constitutionalist bourgeois would care to go), instead of advice to prepare definite ways and means of combating the bourgeoisie when the latter turns against the conquests of the revolution, we are offered a general description of a process, which does not say a word about the concrete aims of *our* activity. The new *Iskra*-ist method of expressing its views reminds one of Marx's opinion (in his famous "theses" on Feuerbach) of the old materialism, which was alien to the ideas of dialectics. The philosophers have only *interpreted* the world, in various ways, said Marx, the point, however, is to *change* it.[19] Similarly, the new *Iskra*-ists can give a tolerable description and explanation of the process of struggle which is taking place before their eyes, but they are altogether incapable of giving a correct slogan for this struggle. Good marchers but bad leaders, they belittle the materialist conception of history by ignoring the active, leading and guiding part in history which can and must be played by parties that understand the material prerequisites of a revolution and that have placed themselves at the head of the progressive classes.

## 5. HOW SHOULD "THE REVOLUTION BE PUSHED FORWARD"?

Let us quote the next section of the resolution:

"Under such conditions, Social-Democracy must strive to maintain during the whole course of the revolution, a position which will best of all secure for it the possibility of pushing the revolution forward, which will not tie the hands of Social-Democracy in its struggle against the inconsistent and self-seeking policy of the bourgeois parties and which will preserve it from being merged in bourgeois democracy.

"Therefore, Social-Democracy must not set itself the aim of seizing or sharing power in the provisional government, but must remain the party of extreme revolutionary opposition."

The advice to occupy a position which best secures the possibility of pushing the revolution forward pleases us very much indeed. We only wish that, in addition to this good advice, they had given a direct indication as to how Social-Democracy should push the revolution further forward right now, in the present political situation, in a period of rumours, conjectures, talk and schemes about the convocation of representatives of the people. Can the revolution be pushed further forward now by one who fails to understand the danger of the *Osvobozhdeniye* theory of "compromise" between the people and the tsar, by one who calls a mere "decision" to convene a constituent assembly a victory, who does not set himself the task of carrying on active propaganda for the idea that a provisional revolutionary government is necessary, or who leaves the slogan of a democratic republic in the shade? Such people actually *push the revolution backward*, because, as far as *practical politics* are concerned, they have halted on the level of the *Osvobozhdentsi*. What is the use of their recognition of a program which demands that the autocracy be replaced by a republic, when in a resolution on tactics that defines the Party's present and immediate tasks in the period of revolution they omit the slogan of a struggle for a republic? Actually it is the position of the *Osvobozhdentsi*, the position of the constitutionalist bourgeoisie, that is now characterized by the fact that the decision to convene a popular constituent assembly is considered a decisive victory, while a prudent silence is maintained on the subject of a provisional revolutionary government and a republic! In order to push the revolution *forward*, i.e., beyond the bounds to which the monarchist bourgeoisie is pushing it, it is necessary actively to advance, emphasize and push to the forefront such slogans as will *preclude* the "inconsistencies" of the bourgeois democrats. At the present time there are *only two* such slogans: 1) a provisional revolutionary government, and 2) a republic, since the slogan of a popular constituent assembly *has been accepted* by the monarchist bourgeoisie (see the program of the Osvobozhdeniye League) and accepted for the very purpose of conjuring away the revolution, of preventing the complete victory of the revolution, and of enabling the big bourgeoisie to strike a huckster's bargain with tsarism. And now we see that of the two slogans which alone are capable of pushing the revolution forward, the Conference completely forgot the slogan of a republic, and plainly put the slogan of a provisional revolutionary government on a par with the *Osvobozhdeniye* slogan of a popular constituent assembly, calling both the one and the other "a decisive victory of the revolution"!!

Yes, such is the undoubted fact, which, we are sure, will serve as a landmark for the future historian of the Russian Social-Democratic movement. The Conference of Social-Democrats held in May 1905 passed a resolution which contains fine words about the necessity of pushing the democratic revolution forward, but which actually pushes it backward, which actually goes no further than the democratic slogans of the monarchist bourgeoisie.

The new *Iskra*-ists like to accuse us of ignoring the danger of the proletariat becoming dissolved in the democratic bourgeoisie. We should like to see the person who would undertake to prove this charge on the basis of the text of the resolutions passed by the Third Congress of the Russian Social-Democratic Labour Party. Our reply to our opponents is: A Social-Democratic Party, operating in a bourgeois society, cannot take part in politics without marching, in one instance or another, *side by side* with the democratic bourgeoisie. The difference between us in this respect is that we march side by side with the revolutionary and republican bourgeoisie, without merging with it, whereas you march side by side with the *liberal and monarchist bourgeoisie*, also without merging with it. *That is how matters stand.*

The tactical slogans you have formulated in the name of the Conference *coincide* with the slogans of the "Constitutional-Democratic" Party, i.e., the *party of the monarchist bourgeoisie*; moreover, you did not even notice or realize this coincidence, thus actually following *at the tail of the Osvobozhdentsi.*

The tactical slogans we have formulated in the name of the Third Congress of the Russian Social-Democratic Labour Party coincide with the slogans of the democratic-revolutionary and republican bourgeoisie. This bourgeoisie and petty bourgeoisie in Russia have not yet formed themselves into a big people's party.* But only a person who is utterly

---

* The Socialist-Revolutionaries are a terrorist group of intellectuals rather than the embryo of such a party, although objectively the activities of that group reduce themselves to this very task of achieving the aims of the revolutionary and republican bourgeoisie.

ignorant of what is now taking place in Russia can doubt the existence of the elements of such a party. We propose to lead (if the course of the great Russian revolution is successful) not only the proletariat, organized by the Social-Democratic Party, but also this petty bourgeoisie, which is capable of marching side by side with us.

In its resolution the Conference unconsciously *descends* to the level of the liberal and monarchist bourgeoisie. The Party Congress in its resolution consciously *raises* to its own level those elements of the revolutionary democracy that are capable of waging a struggle and not of acting as brokers.

Such elements are mostly to be found among the peasants. In classifying the big social groups according to their political tendencies we can, without danger of serious error, identify revolutionary and republican democracy with the mass of the peasants — of course, in the same sense and with the same reservations and implied conditions as we can identify the working class with Social-Democracy. In other words, we can also formulate our conclusions in the following terms: in a revolutionary period the Conference in its *national** *political* slogans unconsciously *descends to the level of the mass of the landlords.* The Party Congress in its national political slogans *raises the peasant masses to the revolutionary level.* We challenge anyone who because of this conclusion may accuse us of evincing a penchant for paradoxes, to refute the proposition that if we are not strong enough to bring the revolution to a successful conclusion, if the revolution *terminates* in a "decisive victory" in the *Osvobozhdentsi* sense, i.e., exclusively in the form of a rep-

* We are not referring here to the special peasant slogans which were dealt with in separate resolutions.

resentative assembly convened by the tsar, which could be called a constituent assembly only in derision — then this will be a revolution in which the *landlord and big bourgeois* element will preponderate. On the other hand, if we are destined to live through a really great revolution, if history prevents a "miscarriage" this time, if we are strong enough to carry the revolution to a successful conclusion, to a decisive victory, not in the *Osvobozhdeniye* or the new *Iskra* sense of the word, then it will be a revolution in which the peasant and proletarian element will preponderate.

Some people may, perhaps, interpret our admission that such a preponderance is possible as a renunciation of the view that the impending revolution will be bourgeois in character. This is very likely, considering how this concept is misused in the *Iskra*. For this reason it will not be at all superfluous to dwell on this question.

## 6. FROM WHAT DIRECTION IS THE PROLETARIAT THREATENED WITH THE DANGER OF HAVING ITS HANDS TIED IN THE STRUGGLE AGAINST THE INCONSISTENT BOURGEOISIE?

Marxists are absolutely convinced of the bourgeois character of the Russian revolution. What does this mean? It means that the democratic reforms in the political system and the social and economic reforms, which have become a necessity for Russia, do not in themselves imply the undermining of capitalism, the undermining of bourgeois rule; on the contrary, they will, for the first time, really clear the ground for a wide and rapid, European, and not Asiatic, development of capitalism; they will, for the first time, make it possible for the bourgeoisie to rule as a class. The Socialist-Revolutionaries cannot grasp this idea, for they are ignorant of the rudiments of the laws of development of commodity and capitalist production; they fail to see that even the complete success of a peasant insurrection, even the redistribution of the whole of the land for the benefit of the peasants and in accordance with their desires ("Black Redistribution" or something of that kind), will not destroy capitalism at all, but will, on the contrary, give an impetus to its development and hasten the class disintegration of the peasantry itself. The failure to grasp this truth makes the Socialist-Revolutionaries unconscious ideologists of the petty bourgeoisie. Insistence on this truth is of enormous importance for Social-Democracy, not only from the theoretical standpoint but also from the standpoint of practical politics, for from it follows that the complete class independence of the party of the proletariat in the present "general democratic" movement is obligatory.

But it does not at all follow from this that a *democratic* revolution (bourgeois in its social and economic substance) is not of *enormous* interest for the proletariat. It does not at all follow from this that the democratic revolution cannot take place in a form advantageous mainly to the big capitalist, the financial magnate and the "enlightened" landlord, as well as in a form advantageous to the peasant and to the worker.

The new *Iskra*-ists thoroughly misunderstand the meaning and significance of the category: bourgeois revolution. Through their arguments there constantly runs the idea that a bourgeois revolution is a revolution which can be advantageous only to the bourgeoisie. And yet nothing is more erroneous than such an idea. A bourgeois revolution is a revolution which does not go beyond the limits of the bourgeois, i.e., capitalist, social and economic system. A bourgeois revolution expresses the need for the development of capitalism, and far from destroying the foundations of capitalism, it does the opposite, it broadens and deepens them. This revolution therefore expresses the interests not only of the working class, but of the entire bourgeoisie as well. Since the rule of the bourgeoisie over the working class is inevitable under capitalism, it is quite correct to say that a bourgeois revolution expresses the interests not so much of the proletariat as of the bourgeoisie. But it is entirely absurd to think that a bourgeois revolution does not express the interests of the proletariat at all. This absurd idea boils down either to the hoary Narodnik theory that a bourgeois revolution runs counter to the interests of the proletariat, and that therefore we do not need bourgeois political liberty; or to anarchism, which rejects all participation of the proletariat in bourgeois politics, in a bourgeois revolution and in bourgeois parliamentarism. From the standpoint of theory, this idea disregards the elementary propositions of Marxism concerning the inevitability of capitalist development where commodity production exists. Marxism teaches that a society which is based on commodity production, and which has commercial intercourse with civilized capitalist nations, at a certain stage of its development, itself, inevitably takes the road of capitalism. Marxism has irrevocably broken with the ravings of the Narodniks and the anarchists to the effect that Russia, for instance, can avoid capitalist development, jump out of capitalism, or skip over it and proceed along some path other than the path of the class struggle on the basis and within the framework of this same capitalism.

43

All these principles of Marxism have been proved and explained over and over again in minute detail in general and with regard to Russia in particular. And from these principles it follows that the idea of seeking salvation for the working class in anything save the further development of capitalism is *reactionary*. In countries like Russia, the working class suffers not so much from capitalism as from the insufficient development of capitalism. The working class is therefore *decidedly interested* in the broadest, freest and most rapid development of capitalism. The removal of all the remnants of the old order which are hampering the broad, free and rapid development of capitalism is of decided *advantage* to the working class. The bourgeois revolution is precisely a revolution that most resolutely sweeps away the survivals of the past, the remnants of serfdom (which include not only autocracy but monarchy as well) and most fully guarantees the broadest, freest and most rapid development of capitalism.

That is why a *bourgeois* revolution is *in the highest degree advantageous to the proletariat*. A bourgeois revolution is *absolutely* necessary in the interests of the proletariat. The more complete and determined, the more consistent the bourgeois revolution, the more assured will be the proletarian struggle against the bourgeoisie for Socialism. Only those who are ignorant of the rudiments of scientific Socialism can regard this conclusion as new or strange, paradoxical. And from this conclusion, among other things, follows the thesis that, *in a certain sense*, a bourgeois revolution is *more advantageous* to the proletariat than to the bourgeoisie. This thesis is unquestionably correct in the following sense: it is to the advantage of the bourgeoisie to rely on certain remnants of the past as against the proletariat, for instance, on

44

the monarchy, the standing army, etc. It is to the advantage of the bourgeoisie if the bourgeois revolution does not too resolutely sweep away all the remnants of the past, but leaves some of them, i.e., if this revolution is not fully consistent, if it is not complete and if it is not determined and relentless. Social-Democrats often express this idea somewhat differently by stating that the bourgeoisie betrays its own self, that the bourgeoisie betrays the cause of liberty, that the bourgeoisie is incapable of being consistently democratic. It is of greater advantage to the bourgeoisie if the necessary changes in the direction of bourgeois democracy take place more slowly, more gradually, more cautiously, less resolutely, by means of reforms and not by means of revolution; if these changes spare the "venerable" institutions of serfdom (such as the monarchy) as much as possible; if these changes develop as little as possible the independent revolutionary activity, initiative and energy of the common people, i.e., the peasantry and especially the workers, for otherwise it will be easier for the workers, as the French say, "to hitch the rifle from one shoulder to the other," i.e., to turn against the bourgeoisie the guns which the bourgeois revolution will place in their hands, the liberty which the revolution will bring, the democratic institutions which will spring up on the ground that is cleared of serfdom.

On the other hand, it is more advantageous for the working class if the necessary changes in the direction of bourgeois democracy take place by way of revolution and not by way of reform; for the way of reform is the way of delay, of procrastination, of the painfully slow decomposition of the putrid parts of the national organism. It is the proletariat and the peasantry that suffer first of all and most of all from their putrefaction. The revolutionary way is the way of quick amputation, which is the least painful to the proletariat, the way of the direct removal of the decomposing parts, the way of fewest concessions to and least consideration for the monarchy and the disgusting, vile, rotten and contaminating institutions which go with it.

So it is not only because of the censorship, not only "for fear of the Jews," that our bourgeois-liberal press deplores the possibility of a revolutionary way, is afraid of revolution, tries to frighten the tsar with the bogey of revolution, is anxious to avoid revolution, grovels and toadies for the sake of miserable reforms as a basis for a reformist way. This standpoint is shared not only by the *Russkiye Vyedomosti, Syn Otechestva, Nasha Zhizn* and *Nashi Dni,* but also by the illegal, uncensored *Osvobozhdeniye.* The very position the bourgeoisie occupies as a class in capitalist society inevitably causes it to be inconsistent in a democratic revolution. The very position the proletariat occupies as a class compels it to be consistently democratic. The bourgeoisie looks backward, fearing democratic progress, which threatens to strengthen the proletariat. The proletariat has nothing to lose but its chains, but with the aid of democracy it has the whole world to gain. That is why the more consistent the bourgeois revolution is in its democratic changes, the less will it limit itself to what is of advantage exclusively to the bourgeoisie. The more consistent the bourgeois revolution, the more does it guarantee the proletariat and the peasantry the benefits accruing from the democratic revolution.

Marxism teaches the proletarian not to keep aloof from the bourgeois revolution, not to be indifferent to it, not to allow the leadership of the revolution to be assumed by the bourgeoisie but, on the contrary, to take a most energetic part in it, to fight most resolutely for consistent proletarian democracy, for carrying the revolution to its conclusion. We cannot jump out of the bourgeois-democratic boundaries of the Russian revolution, but we can vastly extend these boundaries, and within these boundaries we can and must fight for the interests of the proletariat, for its immediate needs and for the conditions that will make it possible to prepare its forces for the future complete victory. There is bourgeois democracy and bourgeois democracy. The Monarch-ist-Zemstvo-ist,[20] who favours an upper chamber, and who "asks" for universal suffrage while secretly, on the sly, striking a bargain with tsarism for a curtailed constitution, is also a bourgeois-democrat. And the peasant who is fight-ing, arms in hand, against the landlords and the government officials and with a "naive republicanism" proposes "to kick out the tsar"* is also a bourgeois-democrat. There are bour-geois-democratic regimes like the one in Germany and also in England, like the one in Austria and also like those in America or Switzerland. He would be a fine Marxist in-deed, who in a period of democratic revolution failed to see the difference between the degrees of democracy, the difference of its various forms and confined himself to "clever" remarks to the effect that, after all, this is "a bour-geois revolution," the fruits of a "bourgeois revolution."

Our new *Iskra*-ists are just such clever fellows flaunting their shortsightedness. They confine themselves to disquisi-tions on the bourgeois character of the revolution just when and where it is necessary to be able to draw a distinction between republican-revolutionary and monarchist-liberal bourgeois democracy, to say nothing of the distinction be-

---

* See the *Osvobozhdeniye*, No. 71, page 337, footnote 2.

tween inconsistent bourgeois democratism and consistent proletarian democratism. They are satisfied — as if they had really become like the "man in the muffler"[21] — to converse dolefully about a "process of mutual struggle of antagonistic classes," when the question is one of giving *democratic leadership* in the present revolution, of emphasizing *progressive democratic* slogans as distinguished from the treacherous slogans of Mr. Struve and Co., of bluntly and straightforwardly stating the immediate aims of the really revolutionary struggle of the proletariat and the peasantry, as distinguished from the liberal haggling of the landlords and factory owners. Such is now the substance of the question, which you, gentlemen, have missed: will our revolution result in a real, immense victory, or merely in a wretched deal, will it go so far as the revolutionary-democratic dictatorship of the proletariat and the peasantry, or will it "peter out" in a liberal constitution à la Shipov?

At first sight it may appear that in raising this question we are deviating entirely from our subject. But this may appear to be so only at first sight. As a matter of fact, it is precisely this question that lies at the root of the difference in principle which has already become clearly marked between the Social-Democratic tactics of the Third Congress of the Russian Social-Democratic Labour Party and the tactics initiated by the Conference of the new *Iskra*-ists. The latter have already taken not two but three steps back, resurrecting the mistakes of Economism in solving problems that are incomparably more complex, more important and more vital to the workers' party, viz., questions of its tactics in time of revolution. That is why we must analyze the question we have raised with all due attention.

The section of the new *Iskra*-ist resolution which we have quoted above points to the danger of Social-Democracy tying its hands in the struggle against the inconsistent policy of the bourgeoisie, of its becoming dissolved in bourgeois democracy. The idea of this danger runs like a thread through all the literature typical of the new *Iskra,* it is the real pivot of the principle involved in our Party split (ever since the elements of squabbling in this split were wholly eclipsed by the elements of a turn towards Economism). And without any equivocation we admit that this danger really exists, that just at the present time, at the height of the Russian revolution, this danger has become particularly grave. The pressing and extremely responsible duty that devolves on all of us theoreticians or — as I should prefer to say of myself — publicists of Social-Democracy, is to find out *from what direction* this danger actually threatens. For the source of our disagreement is not a dispute as to whether such a danger exists, but the dispute as to whether it is caused by the so-called *khvostism* of the "Minority" or the so-called revolutionism of the "Majority."

To obviate all misinterpretations and misunderstandings, let us first of all note that the danger to which we are referring lies not in the subjective, but in the objective aspect of the matter, not in the formal position which Social-Democracy will take in the struggle, but in the material outcome of the entire present revolutionary struggle. The question is not whether this or that Social-Democratic group will want to dissolve in bourgeois democracy or whether they are conscious of the fact that they are merging. Nobody suggests that. We do not suspect any Social-Democrat of harbouring such a desire, and this is not at all a question of desires. Nor is it a question of whether this or that Social-

Democratic group will formally retain its separate identity, individuality and independence of bourgeois democracy throughout the course of the revolution. They may not only proclaim such "independence" but even retain it formally, and yet *it may turn out* that their hands will nonetheless be tied in the struggle against the inconsistency of the bourgeoisie. The final political result of the revolution may prove to be that, in spite of the formal "independence" of Social-Democracy, in spite of its complete organizational individuality as a separate party, it will in fact not be independent, it will not be able to put the imprint of its proletarian independence on the course of events, will prove so weak that, on the whole and in the last analysis, its "dissolving" in the bourgeois democracy will nonetheless be a historical fact.

That is what constitutes the real danger. Now let us see from what direction the danger threatens: from the fact that Social-Democracy as represented by the new *Iskra* is deviating to the Right — as we believe; or from the fact that Social-Democracy as represented by the "Majority," the *Vperyod,* etc., is deviating to the Left — as the new *Iskra*-ists believe.

The answer to this question, as we have pointed out, depends on the objective combination of the actions of the various social forces. The character of these forces has been defined theoretically by the Marxian analysis of Russian life; at the present time it is being defined in practice by the open action of groups and classes in the course of the revolution. Thus, the entire theoretical analysis made by the Marxists long before the period we are now passing through, as well as all the practical observations of the development of revolutionary events, show that from the standpoint of objective conditions there are two possible courses and outcomes of the revolution in Russia. A change in the economic and political system in Russia along bourgeois-democratic lines is inevitable and unavoidable. No power on earth can prevent such a change. But the combined actions of the existing forces which are effecting that change may result in one of two things, may bring about one of two forms of that change. Either 1) the result will be a "decisive victory of the revolution over tsarism," or 2) the forces will be inadequate for a decisive victory and the matter will end in a deal between tsarism and the most "inconsistent" and most "self-seeking" elements of the bourgeoisie. All the infinite variety of detail and combinations, which no one is able to foresee, reduce themselves — in general and on the whole — to either the one or the other of these two outcomes.

Let us now consider these two outcomes, first, from the standpoint of their social significance and, secondly, from the standpoint of the position of Social-Democracy (its "dissolving" or "having its hands tied") in one or the other case.

What is a "decisive victory of the revolution over tsarism"? We have already seen that in using this expression the new *Iskra*-ists fail to grasp even its immediate political significance. Still less do they seem to understand the class essence of this concept. Surely, we Marxists must not under any circumstances allow ourselves to be deluded by *words*, such as "revolution" or "the great Russian revolution," as do many revolutionary democrats (of the Gapon type). We must be perfectly clear in our minds as to what real social forces are opposed to "tsarism" (which is a real force, perfectly intelligible to all) and are capable of gaining a "decisive victory" over it. Such a force cannot be the big bourgeoisie, the landlords, the factory owners, "society" which follows the lead of the *Osvobozhdentsi*. We see that these do not even want a decisive victory. We know that owing to their class position they are incapable of waging a decisive struggle against tsarism; they are too heavily fettered by private property, capital and land to enter into a decisive struggle. They need tsarism with its bureaucratic, police and military forces for use against the proletariat and the peasantry too much to be able to strive for its destruction. No, the only force capable of gaining "a decisive victory over tsarism," is the *people,* i.e., the proletariat and the peasantry, if we take the main, big forces and distribute the rural and urban petty bourgeoisie (also part of "the people") between the two. "A decisive victory of the revolution over tsarism" is the *revolutionary-democratic dictatorship of the proletariat and the peasantry.* Our new *Iskra*-ists cannot escape from this conclusion, which *Vperyod* pointed out long ago. No one else is capable of gaining a decisive victory over tsarism.

And such a victory will be precisely a dictatorship, i.e., it must inevitably rely on military force, on the arming of the masses, on an insurrection, and not on institutions of one kind or another, established in a "lawful" or "peaceful" way. It can be only a dictatorship, for the realization of the changes which are urgently and absolutely indispensable for the proletariat and the peasantry will call forth the desperate resistance of the landlords, of the big bourgeoisie and of tsarism. Without a dictatorship it is impossible to break down that resistance and to repel the counterrevolutionary attempts. But of course it will be a democratic, not a socialist dictatorship. It will not be able (without a series of intermediary stages of revolutionary development) to affect the foundations of capitalism. At best it may bring about a radical redistribution of landed property in favour of the peasantry, establish consistent and full democracy including the formation of a republic, eradicate all the oppressive features of Asiatic bondage, not only in village but also in factory life, lay the foundation for a thorough improvement in the position of the workers and for a rise in their standard of living, and — last but not least — carry the revolutionary conflagration into Europe. Such a victory will by no means as yet transform our bourgeois revolution into a socialist revolution; the democratic revolution will not directly overstep the bounds of bourgeois social and economic relationships; nevertheless, the significance of such a victory for the future development of Russia and of the whole world will be immense. Nothing will raise the revolutionary energy of the world proletariat so much, nothing will shorten the path leading to its complete victory to such an extent, as this decisive victory of the revolution that has now started in Russia.

How far such a victory is probable, is another question. We are not in the least inclined to be unreasonably optimistic on that score, we do not for a moment forget the immense difficulties of this task, but since we are out to fight we must desire victory and be able to point out the right road to it. Tendencies capable of leading to such a victory undoubtedly exist. True, our, Social-Democratic, influence on the masses of the proletariat is as yet very, very inadequate; the revolutionary influence on the mass of the peasantry is altogether insignificant; the proletariat, and especially the peasantry, are still frightfully scattered, backward and ignorant. But revolution unites quickly and enlightens quickly. Every step in its development rouses the masses and attracts them with irresistible force to the side of the revolutionary program, as the only program that fully and consistently expresses their real and vital interests.

According to a law of mechanics, every action produces an equal reaction. In history also the destructive force of a revolution is to a considerable degree dependent on how strong and protracted the suppression of the striving for liberty had been, and how profound the contradiction between the antediluvian "superstructure" and the living forces of the present epoch. The international political situation, too, is in many respects shaping itself in a way most advantageous for the Russian revolution. The insurrection of the workers and peasants has already commenced; it is sporadic, spontaneous, weak, but it unquestionably and undoubtedly proves the existence of forces capable of waging a decisive struggle and marching towards a decisive victory.

If these forces prove inadequate, tsarism will have time to conclude the deal which is already being prepared on two sides, by Messrs. the Bulygins on the one side, and Messrs. the Struves, on the other. Then the whole thing will end in a curtailed constitution, or, if the worst comes to the worst, even in a travesty of a constitution. This will also be a "bourgeois revolution," but it will be a miscarriage, a premature birth, a mongrel. Social-Democracy entertains no illusions on that score, it knows the treacherous nature of the bourgeoisie, it will not lose heart or abandon its persistent, patient, sustained work of giving the proletariat class training even in the most drab, humdrum days of bourgeois-constitutional, "Shipov" bliss. Such an outcome would be more or less similar to the outcome of almost all the democratic revolutions in Europe during the nineteenth century, and our Party development would then proceed along the difficult, hard, long, but familiar and beaten track.

The question now arises: in which of these two possible outcomes will Social-Democracy find its hands actually tied in the fight against the inconsistent and self-seeking bourgeoisie, find itself actually "dissolved," or almost so, in bourgeois democracy?

It is sufficient to put this question clearly to have not a moment's difficulty in answering it.

If the bourgeoisie succeeds in frustrating the Russian revolution by coming to terms with tsarism, Social-Democracy will find its hands actually tied in the fight against the inconsistent bourgeoisie; Social-Democracy will find itself dissolved "in bourgeois democracy" in the sense that the proletariat will not succeed in putting its clear imprint on the revolution, will not succeed in settling accounts with tsarism in the proletarian or, as Marx once said, "in the plebeian" way.

If the revolution gains a decisive victory — then we shall settle accounts with tsarism in the Jacobin, or, if you like, in the plebeian way. "The whole French terrorism," wrote Marx in 1848 in the famous *Neue Rheinische Zeitung,* "was nothing but a plebeian manner of settling accounts with the enemies of the bourgeoisie, with absolutism, feudalism and philistinism" (see Marx, *Nachlass,* Mehring's edition, Vol. III, p. 211).[22] Have those people who, in a period of a democratic revolution, try to frighten the Social-Democratic workers in Russia with the bogey of "Jacobinism" ever stopped to think of the significance of these words of Marx?

The Girondists of contemporary Russian Social-Democracy, the new *Iskra*-ists, do not merge with the *Osvobozhdentsi,* but in point of fact they, by reason of the nature of their slogans, follow at the tail of the latter. And the *Osvobozhdentsi,* i.e., the representatives of the liberal bourgeoisie, wish to settle accounts with the autocracy gently, in a reformist way, in a yielding manner, so as not to offend the aristocracy, the nobles, the Court — cautiously, without breaking anything — kindly and politely, as befits gentlemen in white gloves (like the ones Mr. Petrunkevich borrowed from a bashi-bazouk to wear at the reception of "representatives of the people"[?] held by Nicholas the Bloody. See *Proletary*, No. 5).[23]

The Jacobins of contemporary Social-Democracy — the Bolsheviks, the *Vperyodovtsi, Syezdovtsi, Proletartsi*,[24] or whatever we may call them — wish by their slogans to raise the revolutionary and republican petty bourgeoisie, and especially the peasantry, to the level of the consistent democratism of the proletariat, which fully retains its individuality as a class. They want the people, i.e., the proletariat and the peasantry, to settle accounts with the monarchy and the aristocracy in the "plebeian way," ruthlessly destroying the enemies of liberty, crushing their resistance by force, making no concessions whatever to the accursed heritage of serfdom, of Asiatic barbarism and human degradation.

This, of course, does not mean that we necessarily propose to imitate the Jacobins of 1793, to adopt their views, program, slogans and methods of action. Nothing of the kind. Our program is not an old one, it is a new one — the minimum program of the Russian Social-Democratic Labour Party. We have a new slogan: the revolutionary-democratic dictatorship of the proletariat and the peasantry. We shall also have, if we live to see a real victory of the revolution, new methods of action, in harmony with the nature and aims of the working-class party that is striving for a complete socialist revolution. By our comparison we merely want to explain that the representatives of the progressive class of the twentieth century, of the proletariat, i.e., the Social-Democrats, are divided into two wings (the opportunist and the revolutionary) similar to those into which the representatives of the progressive class of the eighteenth century, the bourgeoisie, were divided, i.e., the Girondists and the Jacobins.

Only in the event of a complete victory of the democratic revolution will the proletariat have its hands free in the struggle against the inconsistent bourgeoisie, only in that event will it not become "dissolved" in bourgeois democracy, but will leave its proletarian or rather proletarian-peasant imprint on the whole revolution.

In a word, in order that it may not find itself with its hands tied in the struggle against the inconsistent bourgeois democrats, the proletariat must be sufficiently class conscious and strong to rouse the peasantry to revolutionary consciousness, to direct its attack, and thereby to pursue the line of consistent proletarian democratism independently.

This is how matters stand with regard to the question, unsatisfactorily answered by the new *Iskra*-ists, of the danger of our hands being tied in the struggle against the inconsistent bourgeoisie. The bourgeoisie will always be inconsistent. There is nothing more naive and futile than attempts to set forth conditions and points,* which if satisfied, would enable us to consider that the bourgeois democrat is a sincere friend of the people. Only the proletariat can be a consistent fighter for democracy. It may become a victorious fighter for democracy only if the peasant masses join its revolutionary

---

* As was attempted by Starover in his resolution, annulled by the Third Congress,[25] and as is attempted by the Conference in an equally bad resolution.

struggle. If the proletariat is not strong enough for this, the bourgeoisie will be at the head of the democratic revolution and will impart to it an inconsistent and self-seeking nature. Nothing short of a revolutionary-democratic dictatorship of the proletariat and the peasantry can prevent this.

Thus, we arrive at the undoubted conclusion that it is precisely the new *Iskra*-ists' tactics, by reason of their objective significance, that are *playing into the hands of the bourgeois democrats.* Preaching organizational diffusion that goes to the length of plebiscites, the principle of compromise and the divorcement of Party literature from the Party, belittling the aims of armed insurrection, confusing the popular political slogans of the revolutionary proletariat with those of the monarchist bourgeoisie, distorting the requisites for a "decisive victory of the revolution over tsarism" — all this taken together constitutes that very policy of *khvostism* in a revolutionary period which perplexes the proletariat, disorganizes it, confuses its understanding and belittles the tactics of Social-Democracy, instead of pointing out the only way to victory and of rallying all the revolutionary and republican elements of the people to the slogan of the proletariat.

---

In order to confirm this conclusion, at which we have arrived on the basis of an analysis of the resolution, let us approach this same question from other angles. Let us see, first, how a simple and outspoken Menshevik illustrates the new *Iskra* tactics in the Georgian *Sotsial-Demokrat*. And, secondly, let us see who is actually making use of the new *Iskra* slogans in the present political situation.

## 7. THE TACTICS OF "ELIMINATING
## THE CONSERVATIVES FROM
## THE GOVERNMENT"

The article in the organ of the Tiflis Menshevik "Committee" (*Sotsial-Demokrat*, No. 1) to which we have just referred is entitled "The Zemsky Sobor and Our Tactics." Its author has not yet entirely forgotten our program; he advances the slogan of a republic, but this is how he discusses tactics:

> "It is possible to point to two ways of achieving this goal" (a republic): "either completely ignore the Zemsky Sobor that is being convened by the government and defeat the government by force of arms, form a revolutionary government and convene a constituent assembly, or declare the Zemsky Sobor the centre of our actions, influencing its composition and activity by force of arms and either forcibly compelling it to declare itself a constituent assembly or convening a constituent assembly through it. These two tactics differ very sharply from one another. Let us see which of them is more advantageous to us."

This is how the Russian new *Iskra*-ists set forth the ideas that were subsequently incorporated in the resolution we have analyzed. Note that this was written before the battle of Tsushima, when the Bulygin "scheme" had not yet seen the light of the day. Even the liberals were losing patience and expressing their lack of confidence in the pages of the legal press; but a new *Iskra*-ist Social-Democrat proved more credulous than the liberals. He declares that the Zemsky Sobor "is being convened" and trusts the tsar so much that he proposes to make this as yet non-existent Zemsky Sobor (or, possibly, "State Duma" or "Advisory Legislative Assembly"?) the centre of our actions. Being more outspoken and straightforward than the authors of the resolution adopted at the Conference, our Tiflisian does not put the two "tactics" (which he expounds with inimitable naïveté) on a par, but declares that the second is more "advantageous." Just listen:

> "The first tactics. As you know, the coming revolution is a bourgeois revolution, i.e., its purpose is to effect such changes in the present system as are of interest not only to the proletariat but to the whole of bourgeois society. All classes are opposed to the government, even the capitalists themselves. The militant proletariat and the militant bourgeoisie are in a certain sense marching together and jointly attacking the autocracy from different sides. The government is completely isolated and lacks public sympathy. For this reason it is very easy to destroy it. The Russian proletariat as a whole is not yet sufficiently class conscious and organized to be able to carry out the revolution by itself. And even if it were able to do so, it would carry through a proletarian (socialist) revolution and not a bourgeois revolution. Hence, it is in our interest that the government remain without allies, that it be unable to disunite the opposition, unable to ally the bourgeoisie to itself and leave the proletariat isolated. . . ."

So, it is in the interests of the proletariat that the tsarist government shall not be able to disunite the bourgeoisie and the proletariat! Is it not by mistake that this Georgian organ is called *Sotsial-Demokrat* instead of *Osvobozhdeniye*? And note its peerless philosophy of democratic revolution! Is it not obvious that this poor Tiflisian is hopelessly confused by the pedantic *khvostist* interpretation of the concept "bourgeois revolution"? He discusses the question of the possible isolation of the proletariat in a democratic revolution and *forgets* . . . forgets about a trifle . . . about the peasantry! Of the possible allies of the proletariat he knows and favours the landowning Zemstvo-ists and is not aware of the peasants. And this in the Caucasus! Well, were we not right when we said that by its method of reasoning the new *Iskra* was sinking to the level of the monarchist bourgeoisie instead of raising the revolutionary peasantry to the position of our ally?

". . . Otherwise the defeat of the proletariat and the victory of the government is inevitable. This is just what the autocracy is striving for. In its Zemsky Sobor it will undoubtedly attract to its side the representatives of the nobility, of the Zemstvos, the cities, the universities and similar bourgeois institutions. It will try to appease them with petty concessions and thereby reconcile them to itself. Strengthened in this way, it will direct all its blows against the working people who will have been isolated. It is our duty to prevent such an unfortunate outcome. But can this be done by the first method? Let us assume that we paid no attention whatever to the Zemsky Sobor, but started to prepare for insurrection ourselves, and one fine day came out in the streets armed and ready for battle. The result would be that we would be confronted not with one but with two enemies: the government and the Zemsky Sobor. While we were preparing, they would manage to come to terms, enter into an agreement with one another, draw up a constitution advantageous to themselves and divide power between them. These tactics are of direct advantage to the government, and we must reject them in the most energetic fashion. . . ."

Now this is frank! We must resolutely reject the "tactics" of preparing an insurrection because "while we were preparing" the government would come to terms with the bourgeoisie! Can one find in the old literature of the most rabid "Economism" anything that would even approximate such a disgrace to revolutionary Social-Democracy? That insurrections and outbreaks of workers and peasants are occurring, first in one place and then in another, is a fact. The Zemsky Sobor, however, is a Bulygin promise. And the *Sotsial-Demokrat* of the city of Tiflis decides: to reject the tactics of preparing an insurrection and to wait for a "centre of influence" — the Zemsky Sobor. . . .

". . . The second tactics, on the contrary, consist in placing the Zemsky Sobor under our surveillance, in not giving it the opportunity to act according to its own will and enter into an agreement with the government.*

"We support the Zemsky Sobor to the extent that it fights the autocracy, and we fight it in those cases when it becomes reconciled with the autocracy. By energetic interference and force we shall cause a split among the deputies,** rally the radicals to our side, eliminate the conservatives from the government and thus put the whole Zemsky Sobor on the path of revolution. Thanks to such tactics the government will always remain isolated, the opposition strong and the establishment of a democratic system will thereby be facilitated."

Well, well! Let anyone now say that we exaggerate the new *Iskra*-ists' turn to the most vulgar semblance of Economism. This is positively like the famous powder for exterminating flies: you catch the fly, sprinkle it with the powder and the fly will die. Split the deputies of the Zemsky Sobor by *force,* "eliminate the conservatives from the government" — and the *whole* Zemsky Sobor will take *the path of revolution* .... No "Jacobin" armed insurrection of any sort, but just like that, in genteel, almost parliamentary fashion, "influencing" *the members of the Zemsky Sobor.*

Poor Russia! It has been said that she always wears the old-fashioned bonnets that Europe discards. We have no parliament as yet, even Bulygin has not yet promised one, but we have any amount of parliamentary cretinism.[26]

". . . How should this interference be effected? First of all, we shall demand that the Zemsky Sobor be convened on the basis of universal and equal suffrage, direct elections and secret ballot. Simultaneously with the announcement*** of this method of election, complete freedom

---

* By what means can the Zemstvo-ists be deprived of their own will? Perhaps by the use of a special sort of litmus paper?

** Heavens! This is certainly rendering tactics "profound"! There are no forces available to fight in the streets, but it is possible "to split the deputies" "by force." Listen, comrade from Tiflis, one may prevaricate, but one should know the limit. . . .

*** In *Iskra?*

62

to carry on the election campaign, i.e., freedom of assembly, of speech and of the press, the inviolability of the electors and the candidates and the release of all political prisoners must be made law.* The elections themselves must be fixed as late as possible so that we have sufficient time to inform and prepare the people. And since the drafting of the regulations governing the convocation of the Sobor has been entrusted to a commission headed by Bulygin, Minister of the Interior, we should also exert pressure on this commission and on its members.** If the Bulygin Commission refuses to satisfy our demands*** and grants suffrage only to property owners, then we must interfere in these elections and, by revolutionary means, force the voters to elect progressive candidates and in the Zemsky Sobor demand a constituent assembly. Finally, we must, by all possible measures: demonstrations, strikes and insurrection if need be, compel the Zemsky Sobor to convene a constituent assembly or declare itself to be such. The armed proletariat must constitute itself the defender of the constituent assembly, and both together**** will march forward to a democratic republic.

"Such are the Social-Democratic tactics, and they alone will secure us victory."

Let not the reader imagine that this incredible nonsense is simply a maiden attempt at writing on the part of some new *Iskra* adherent with no authority or influence. No, this is what is stated in the *organ* of an entire committee of new *Iskra*-ists, the Tiflis Committee. More than that. This nonsense has been *openly endorsed by the "Iskra"* in No. 100 of which we read the following about that issue of the *Sotsial-Demokrat*:

*"The first issue is edited in a lively and talented manner. The experienced hand of a capable editor and publicist is perceptible. . . . It may be said with all confidence that*

---

* By Nicholas?

** So this is what is meant by the tactics of "eliminating the conservatives from the government"!

*** But surely such a thing cannot happen if we follow these correct and profound tactics!

**** Both the armed proletariat and the conservatives "eliminated from the government"?

*the newspaper will brilliantly carry out the task it has set itself."*

Yes! If that task is clearly to show all and sundry the utter ideological decay of new *Iskra*-ism, then it has indeed been carried out "brilliantly." No one could have expressed the new *Iskra*-ists' degradation to liberal bourgeois opportunism in a more "lively, talented and capable" manner.

## 8. *OSVOBOZHDENIYE*-ISM AND NEW *ISKRA*-ISM

Let us now proceed to another striking confirmation of the political meaning of new *Iskra*-ism.

In a splendid, remarkable and most instructive article, entitled "How to Find Oneself" (*Osvobozhdeniye*, No. 71), Mr. Struve wages war against the "programmatic revolutionism" of our extreme parties. Mr. Struve is particularly displeased with me personally.* As for myself, Mr. Struve

---

* "In comparison with the revolutionism of Messrs. Lenin and associates, the revolutionism of the West-European Social-Democracy of Bebel, and even of Kautsky, is opportunism; but the foundations of even this already toned down revolutionism have been undermined and washed away by history." A most irate thrust. Only Mr. Struve is mistaken in thinking that it is possible to pile everything on to me, as if I were dead. It is sufficient for me to issue a challenge to Mr. Struve, which he will never be able to accept. When and where did I call the "revolutionism of Bebel and Kautsky" opportunism? When and where did I ever claim to have created any sort of special trend in International Social-Democracy *not identical* with the trend of Bebel and Kautsky? When and where have there been brought to light differences between me, on the one hand, and Bebel and Kautsky, on the other — differences even slightly approximating in seriousness the differences between Bebel and Kautsky, for instance, on the agrarian question in Breslau?[27] Let Mr. Struve try to answer these three questions.

And to our readers we say: The liberal bourgeoisie *everywhere* and *always* has recourse to the method of assuring its adherents in a given

could not please me more: I could not wish for a better ally in the fight against the renascent Economism of the new *Iskra*-ists and the utter lack of principle displayed by the "Socialist-Revolutionaries." On some other occasion we shall relate how Mr. Struve and the *Osvobozhdeniye* proved in practice how utterly reactionary are the "amendments" to Marxism made in the draft program of the Socialist-Revolutionaries. We have already repeatedly spoken about how Mr. Struve rendered me honest, faithful and real service every time he approved of the new *Iskra*-ists *in principle*\* and we shall say so once more now.

---

country that the Social-Democrats of that country are the most unreasonable, whereas their comrades in a neighbouring country are "good boys." The German bourgeoisie has held up those "good boys" of French Socialists as models for the Bebels and the Kautskys *hundreds of times*. The French bourgeoisie quite recently pointed to the "good boy" Bebel as a model for the French Socialists. It is an old trick, Mr. Struve! You will find only children and ignoramuses swallowing that bait. The complete unanimity of international revolutionary Social-Democracy on all major questions of program and tactics is a most incontrovertible fact.

\* Let us remind the reader that the article "What Should Not Be Done?" (*Iskra*, No. 52) was hailed with noise and clamour by the *Osvobozhdeniye* as a "noteworthy turn" towards concessions to the opportunists. The trends of the principles behind the new *Iskra* ideas were especially lauded by the *Osvobozhdeniye* in an item on the split among the Russian Social-Democrats. Commenting on Trotsky's pamphlet, "Our Political Tasks," the *Osvobozhdeniye* pointed out the similarity between the ideas of this author and what was once written and said by the *Rabocheye Dyelo*-ists Krichevsky, Martynov, Akimov (see the leaflet entitled "An Obliging Liberal" published by the *Vperyod*). The *Osvobozhdeniye* welcomed Martynov's pamphlet on the two dictatorships (see the item in the *Vperyod*, No. 9). Finally Starover's belated complaints about the old slogan of the old *Iskra*, "first draw a line of demarcation and then unite," met with special sympathy on the part of the *Osvobozhdeniye*.

Mr. Struve's article contains a number of very interesting statements, which we can note here only in passing. He intends "to create Russian democracy by relying on class collaboration and not on class struggle," in which case "the socially privileged intelligentsia" (something in the nature of the "cultured nobility" to which Mr. Struve makes obeisance with the grace of a truly high-society . . . lackey) will bring the weight of its "social position" (the weight of its moneybags) to this "non-class" party. Mr. Struve expresses the desire to show the youth the worthlessness "of the hackneyed radical opinion that the bourgeoisie has become frightened and has sold out the proletariat and the cause of liberty." (We welcome this desire with all our heart. Nothing will confirm the correctness of this Marxian "hackneyed" opinion better than a war waged against it by Mr. Struve. Please, Mr. Struve, don't pigeonhole this splendid plan of yours!)

For the purposes of our subject it is important to note the *practical* slogans against which this politically sensitive representative of the Russian bourgeoisie, who is so responsive to the slightest change in the weather, is fighting at the present time. First, he is fighting against the slogan of republicanism. Mr. Struve is firmly convinced that this slogan is "incomprehensible and foreign to the masses of the people" (he forgets to add: comprehensible, but not of advantage to the bourgeoisie!). We should like to see what reply Mr. Struve would get from the workers in our study circles and at our mass meetings! Or are the workers not the people? And the peasants? They are given to what Mr. Struve calls "naive republicanism" ("to kick out the tsar") — but the liberal bourgeoisie believes that *naive* republicanism will be replaced not by enlightened republicanism but by enlightened monarchism! Ça dépend, Mr. Struve; it will depend on circumstances. Neither tsarism nor the bourgeoisie can help opposing a radical improvement in the condition of the peasantry at the expense of the landed estates, whereas the working class cannot help assisting the peasantry in this respect.

Secondly, Mr. Struve assures us that "in a civil war the attacking party always proves to be in the wrong." This idea verges closely on the above-mentioned trends of the new *Iskra* ideas. We will not say, of course, that in civil war it is *always* advantageous to attack; no, sometimes defensive tactics are obligatory *for a time*. But to apply a proposition like the one Mr. Struve has made to Russia in 1905 means precisely displaying a little of the "hackneyed radical opinion" ("the bourgeoisie takes fright and betrays the cause of liberty"). Whoever now refuses to attack the autocracy and reaction, whoever is not making preparations for such an attack, whoever is not advocating it, takes the name of adherent of the revolution in vain.

Mr. Struve condemns the slogans: "secrecy" and "rioting" (a riot being "an insurrection in miniature"). Mr. Struve spurns both the one and the other — and he does so from the standpoint of "approaching the masses." We should like to ask Mr. Struve whether he can point to any passage in, for instance, *What Is To Be Done?* — the work of an extreme revolutionary from his standpoint — which advocates rioting. As regards "secrecy" is there really much difference between, for example, us and Mr. Struve? Are we not both working on "illegal" newspapers which are being smuggled into Russia "secretly" and which serve the "secret" groups of either the Osvobozhdeniye League or the R.S.D.L.P.? Our workers' mass meetings are often held "secretly" — that sin does exist. But what about the meetings of the gentlemen of the Osvobozhdeniye League? Is there any reason why you should brag, Mr. Struve, and look down upon the despised partisans of despised secrecy?

True, the supplying of arms to the workers demands strict secrecy. On this point Mr. Struve is rather more outspoken. Just listen: "As regards armed insurrection, or a revolution in the technical sense, only mass propaganda in favour of a democratic program can create the social-psychological conditions for a general armed insurrection. Thus, even from the point of view that an armed insurrection is the *inevitable* consummation of the present struggle for emancipation — a view I do not share — the permeation of the masses with ideas of democratic reform is a most fundamental and most necessary task."

Mr. Struve tries to evade the issue. He speaks of the inevitability of an insurrection instead of speaking about its necessity for the victory of the revolution. The insurrection — unprepared, spontaneous, sporadic — has already begun. No one can positively vouch that it will develop into an entire and integral popular armed insurrection, for that depends on the state of the revolutionary forces (which can be fully gauged only in the course of the struggle itself), on the behaviour of the government and the bourgeoisie, and on a number of other circumstances which it is impossible to estimate exactly. There is no point in speaking about inevitability, in the sense of absolute certainty with regard to some definite event, as Mr. Struve does. What you must discuss, if you want to be a partisan of the revolution is whether insurrection is *necessary for the victory* of the revolution, whether it is necessary to proclaim it vigorously, to advocate and make immediate and energetic preparations for it. Mr. Struve cannot fail to understand this difference: he does not, for instance, obscure the question of the necessity of universal suffrage — which is indisputable for a democrat — by raising the question of whether its attainment is inevitable in the course of the present revolution — which is debatable and of no urgency for people engaged in political activity. By evading the issue of the necessity of an insurrection, Mr. Struve expresses the innermost essence of the political position of the liberal bourgeoisie. In the first place, the bourgeoisie would prefer to come to terms with the autocracy rather than crush it; secondly, the bourgeoisie in any case thrusts the armed struggle upon the shoulders of the workers. This is the *real* meaning of Mr. Struve's evasiveness. That is why he *backs out* of the question of the necessity of an insurrection towards the question of the "social-psychological conditions" for it, of preliminary "propaganda." Just as the bourgeois windbags in the Frankfurt Parliament of 1848 engaged in drawing up resolutions, declarations and decisions, in "mass propaganda" and in preparing the "social-psychological conditions" at a time when it was a matter of repelling the armed force of the government, when the movement "led to the necessity" for an armed struggle, when verbal persuasion alone (which is a hundredfold necessary during the preparatory period) became banal, bourgeois inactivity and cowardice — so also Mr. Struve evades the question of insurrection, screening himself behind *phrases*. Mr. Struve vividly shows us what many Social-Democrats stubbornly fail to see, namely, that a revolutionary period differs from ordinary, everyday preparatory periods in history in that the temper, excitement and convictions of the masses must and do reveal themselves in *action*.

Vulgar revolutionism fails to see that the word is also a deed; this proposition is indisputable when applied to history *generally*, or to those periods of history when no open political mass actions take place, and when they cannot be replaced or artificially evoked by putsches of any sort. *Khvostist* revolutionaries fail to understand that — when a revolutionary period has started, when the old "superstructure" has cracked from top to bottom, when open political action on the part of the classes and masses who are creating a new superstructure for themselves has become a fact, when civil war has begun — then, to confine oneself to "words" *as of old,* and fail to advance the *direct slogan* to pass to "deeds," still to try avoid deeds by pleading the need for "psychological conditions" and "propaganda" in general, is apathy, lifelessness, pedantry, or else betrayal of the revolution and treachery to it. The Frankfurt windbags of the democratic bourgeoisie are a memorable historical example of just such treachery, or of just such pedantic stupidity.

Would you like an explanation of this difference between vulgar revolutionism and the *khvostism* of revolutionaries by an example taken from the history of the Social-Democratic movement in Russia? We shall give you such an explanation. Call to mind the years 1901 and 1902, which are so recent but which already seem ancient history to us today. Demonstrations had begun. The protagonists of vulgar revolutionism raised a cry about "storming" (*Rabo-*

*cheye Dyelo),*[28] "bloodthirsty leaflets" were issued (of Berlin origin, if my memory does not fail me), attacks were made on the "literature writing" and armchair nature of the idea of conducting agitation on a national scale through a newspaper (Nadezhdin).[29] On the other hand, the *khvostism* of revolutionaries was revealed in preaching that "the economic struggle is the *best* means of political agitation." What was the attitude of the revolutionary Social-Democrats? They attacked both these trends. They condemned flash-in-the-pan methods and the cries about storming, for it was or should have been obvious to all that open mass action was a matter of the days to come. They condemned *khvostism* and bluntly issued the slogan *even* of a popular armed insurrection, not in the sense of a direct appeal (Mr. Struve would not discover any appeals to "riots" in our utterances of that period), but in the sense of a *necessary* deduction, in the sense of "propaganda" (about which Mr. Struve has bethought himself only now — our honourable Mr. Struve is always several years behind the times), in the sense of preparing those very "social-psychological conditions" about which the representatives of the bewildered, huckstering bourgeoisie are now holding forth "sadly and inappropriately." *At that time* propaganda and agitation, agitation and propaganda, were really pushed to the fore by the objective state of affairs. *At that time* the work of publishing an all-Russian political newspaper, the weekly issuance of which was regarded as an ideal, could be proposed (and was proposed in *What Is To Be Done?*) as the touchstone of the work of preparing for an insurrection. *At that time* the slogans advocating mass agitation *instead of* direct armed action, preparation of the

71

social-psychological conditions for insurrection *instead of* flash-in-the-pan methods, were the only correct slogans for the revolutionary Social-Democratic movement. *At the present time* the slogans have been superseded by events, the movement has gone beyond them, they have become castoffs, rags fit only to clothe the hypocrisy of the *Osvobozhdeniye* and the *khvostism* of the new *Iskra*!

Or perhaps I am mistaken? Perhaps the revolution has not yet begun? Perhaps the time for open political action of classes has not yet arrived? Perhaps there is still no civil war, and the criticism of weapons should not as yet be the *necessary* and obligatory successor, heir, trustee and wielder of the weapon of criticism?

Look around, poke your head out of your study and look into the street for an answer. Has not the government itself started civil war by shooting down hosts of peaceful and unarmed citizens everywhere? Are not the armed Black Hundreds acting as "arguments" of the autocracy? Has not the bourgeoisie — even the bourgeoisie — recognized the need for a citizens' militia? Does not Mr. Struve himself, the ideally moderate and punctilious Mr. Struve, say (alas, he says so only to evade the issue!) that "the open nature of revolutionary action" (that's the sort of fellows we are today!) "is now one of the most important conditions for exerting an educational influence upon the masses of the people"?

Those who have eyes to see can have no doubt as to how the question of armed insurrection must be presented by the partisans of revolution at the present time. Just take a look at the *three* ways in which this question has been presented in the organs of the free press which are at all capable of influencing the *masses*.

72

The first presentation. The resolution of the Third Congress of the Russian Social-Democratic Labour Party.* It is publicly acknowledged and declared that the general democratic revolutionary movement *has already led to the ne-*

---

* The following is the text in full:

*"Whereas*

"1. the proletariat, being, by virtue of its very position, the most advanced and the only consistently revolutionary class, is for that very reason called upon to play the leading part in the general democratic revolutionary movement in Russia;

"2. this movement has already brought about the necessity of an armed insurrection;

"3. the proletariat will inevitably take a most energetic part in this insurrection, this participation determining the fate of the revolution in Russia;

"4. the proletariat can play the leading part in this revolution only if it is welded into a united and independent political force under the banner of the Social-Democratic Labour Party, which is to guide its struggle not only ideologically but practically as well;

"5. it is only by fulfilling this part that the proletariat can be assured of the most favourable conditions for the struggle for Socialism against the propertied classes of a bourgeois-democratic Russia;

"the Third Congress of the R.S.D.L.P. recognizes that the task of organizing the proletariat for direct struggle against the autocracy through armed insurrection is one of the most important and pressing tasks of the Party in the present revolutionary period.

"The Congress therefore resolves to instruct all the Party organizations:

"a) to explain to the proletariat by means of propaganda and agitation not only the political importance, but also the practical organizational aspect of the impending armed insurrection;

"b) in this propaganda and agitation to explain the part played by mass political strikes, which may be of great importance at the beginning and in the very process of the insurrection;

"c) to adopt the most energetic measures to arm the proletariat and also to draw up a plan for the armed insurrection and for direct leadership of the latter, establishing for this purpose, to the extent that it is necessary, special groups of Party functionaries." [Author's note to the 1907 edition.]

*cessity* of an armed insurrection. The organization of the proletariat for an insurrection has been placed on the order of the day as one of the essential, principal and *indispensable* tasks of the Party. Instructions are issued to adopt the *most energetic* measures to arm the proletariat and to ensure the possibility of directly leading the insurrection.

The second presentation. An article in the *Osvobozhdeniye,* containing a statement of principles, by the "leader of the Russian constitutionalists" (as Mr. Struve was recently described by such an influential organ of the European bourgeoisie as the *Frankfurter Zeitung*), or the leader of the Russian progressive bourgeoisie. He does not share the opinion that an insurrection is inevitable. Secret activity and riots are the specific methods of irrational revolutionism. Republicanism is a method of stunning. The question of armed insurrection is really a mere technical question, whereas "the fundamental and most necessary task" is to carry on mass propaganda and to prepare the social-psychological conditions.

The third presentation. The resolution of the new *Iskra*-ist Conference. Our task is to prepare an insurrection. A planned insurrection is out of the question. Favourable conditions for an insurrection are created by the disorganization of the government, by our agitation, and by our organization. Only then "can technical military preparations acquire more or less serious significance."

And is that all? Yes, that is all. The new *Iskra*-ist leaders of the proletariat still do not know whether insurrection has become a necessity. It is still not clear to them whether the task of organizing the proletariat for direct battle has become an urgent one. It is not necessary to urge the adoption of the most energetic measures; it is far more important (in 1905, and not in 1902) to explain in general outlines under what conditions these measures "may" acquire "more or less serious" significance. . . .

Do you see now, comrades of the new *Iskra,* where your turn to Martynovism has led you? Do you realize that your political philosophy has proved to be a rehash of the *Osvobozhdeniye* philosophy? — that (against your will and without your being aware of it) you are following at the tail of the monarchist bourgeoisie? Is it clear to you now that, while repeating what you have learned by rote and attaining perfection in sophistry, you have lost sight of the fact that — in the memorable words of Peter Struve's memorable article — "the open nature of revolutionary *action* is now one of the most important conditions for exerting an educational influence upon the masses of the people"?

## 9. WHAT DOES BEING A PARTY OF EXTREME OPPOSITION IN TIME OF REVOLUTION MEAN?

Let us return to the resolution on a provisional government. We have shown that the tactics of the new *Iskra*-ists do not push the revolution forward — which they may have wanted to make possible by their resolution — but back. We have shown that it is precisely these tactics that *tie the hands* of Social-Democracy in the struggle against the inconsistent bourgeoisie and do not safeguard it against being dissolved in bourgeois democracy. Naturally, the false premises of the resolution lead to the false conclusion that: "Therefore, Social-Democracy must not set itself the aim of seizing or sharing power in the provisional government, but

75

must remain the party of extreme revolutionary opposition." Consider the first half of this conclusion, which is part of a statement of aims. Do the new *Iskra*-ists declare the aim of Social-Democratic activity to be a decisive victory of the revolution over tsarism? They do. They are unable correctly to formulate the requisites for a decisive victory and stray into the *Osvobozhdeniye* formulation, but they do set themselves the aforementioned aim. Further: do they connect a provisional government with insurrection? Yes, they do so plainly, by stating that a provisional government "will emerge from a victorious popular insurrection." Finally, do they set themselves the aim of leading the insurrection? Yes, they do. Like Mr. Struve, they do not admit that an insurrection is an urgent necessity, but at the same time, unlike Mr. Struve, they say that "Social-Democracy strives to *subject* it" (the insurrection) "to its influence and *leadership* and to use it in the interests of the working class."

How nicely this hangs together, does it not? We set ourselves the *aim* of subjecting the insurrection of both the proletarian and *non-proletarian* masses to our influence and our leadership, and of using it in our interests. Hence, we set ourselves the aim of leading, in the insurrection, both the proletariat and the revolutionary bourgeoisie and petty bourgeoisie ("the non-proletarian groups"), i.e., of *"sharing"* the leadership of the insurrection between the Social-Democracy and the revolutionary bourgeoisie. We set ourselves the aim of securing *victory* for the insurrection, which is to lead to the establishment of a provisional government ("which will emerge from a victorious popular insurrection"). *Therefore* ... therefore we must not set ourselves the aim of seizing power or of sharing it in a provisional revolutionary government!!

Our friends cannot dovetail their arguments. They vacillate between the standpoint of Mr. Struve, who is evading the issue of an insurrection, and the standpoint of revolutionary Social-Democracy, which calls upon us to undertake this urgent task. They vacillate between anarchism, which on principle condemns all participation in a provisional revolutionary government as treachery to the proletariat, and Marxism, which demands such participation on condition that the Social-Democratic Party exercises the leading influence in the insurrection.* They have no independent position whatever: neither that of Mr. Struve, who wants to come to terms with tsarism and is therefore compelled to resort to evasions and subterfuges on the question of insurrection, nor that of the anarchists, who condemn all action "from above" and all participation in a bourgeois revolution. The new *Iskra*-ists confuse a deal with tsarism with a victory over tsarism. They want to take part in a bourgeois revolution. They have gone somewhat beyond Martynov's *Two Dictatorships*. They even consent to lead the insurrection of the people — in order to renounce that leadership immediately after victory is won (or, perhaps, immediately before the victory?), i.e., *in order not to avail themselves of the fruits of victory* but to turn all these fruits over *entirely to the bourgeoisie*. This is what they call "using the insurrection in the interests of the working class...."

There is no need to dwell on this muddle any longer. It will be more useful to examine how this muddle *originated* in the formulation which reads: "to remain the party of extreme revolutionary opposition."

---

* See *Proletary*, No. 3, "On the Provisional Revolutionary Government," article two. (V. I. Lenin, *Collected Works*, 4th Russ. ed., Vol. VIII, pp. 440-47. — *Ed.*)

This is one of the familiar propositions of international revolutionary Social-Democracy. It is a perfectly correct proposition. It has become a commonplace for all opponents of revisionism or opportunism in parliamentary countries. It has become generally accepted as the legitimate and necessary rebuff to "parliamentary cretinism," Millerandism, Bernsteinism[30] and the Italian reformism of the Turati brand. Our good new *Iskra*-ists have learned this excellent proposition by heart and are zealously applying it . . . *quite inappropriately*. Categories of the parliamentary struggle are introduced into resolutions written for conditions in which no parliament exists. The concept "opposition," which has become the reflection and the expression of a political situation in which no one seriously speaks of an *insurrection*, is senselessly applied to a situation in which insurrection *has begun* and in which all the supporters of the revolution are thinking and talking about leadership in it. The desire to *"stick to"* old methods, i.e., action only "from below," is expressed with pomp and clamour *precisely at a time* when the revolution has confronted us with the necessity, in the event of the insurrection being victorious, of acting *from above*.

No, our new *Iskra*-ists are decidedly out of luck! Even when they formulate a correct Social-Democratic proposition they don't know how to apply it correctly. They failed to take into consideration that in a period in which a revolution has begun, when there is no parliament, when there is civil war, when insurrectionary outbreaks occur, the concepts and terms of parliamentary struggle are changed and transformed into their opposites. They failed to take into consideration the fact that, under the circumstances referred to, amendments are moved by means of street demonstrations, interpellations are introduced by means of offensive action by armed citizens, opposition to the government is effected by forcibly overthrowing the government.

Like the well-known hero of our folklore, who repeated good advice just when it was inappropriate, our admirers of Martynov repeat the lessons of peaceful parliamentarism just at a time when, as they themselves state, actual hostilities have commenced.   There is nothing more ridiculous than this pompous emphasis of the slogan "extreme opposition" in a resolution which begins by referring to a "decisive victory of the revolution" and to a "popular insurrection"! Try to visualize, gentlemen, what it means to be the "extreme opposition" in a period of insurrection. Does it mean exposing the government or deposing it?   Does it mean voting against the government or defeating its armed forces in open battle?   Does it mean refusing the government replenishments for its exchequer or the revolutionary seizure of this exchequer in order to use it for the requirements of the uprising, to arm the workers and peasants and to convoke a constituent assembly?   Are you not beginning to understand, gentlemen, that the term "extreme opposition" expresses only negative actions — to expose, to vote against, to refuse?   Why is this so?   Because this term applies only to the parliamentary struggle and, moreover, to a period when no one makes "decisive victory" the immediate object of the struggle.   Are you not beginning to understand that things undergo a cardinal change in this respect from the moment the politically oppressed people launch a determined attack along the whole front in desperate struggle for victory?

The workers ask us:  Is it necessary energetically to take up the urgent business of insurrection?  What is to be done to make the incipient insurrection victorious? What use should be made of the victory? What program can and should then be applied? The new *Iskra*-ists, who are making Marxism more profound, answer: We must remain the party of extreme revolutionary opposition. . . . Well, were we not right in calling these knights past masters in philistinism?

## 10. "REVOLUTIONARY COMMUNES" AND THE REVOLUTIONARY-DEMOCRATIC DICTATORSHIP OF THE PROLETARIAT AND THE PEASANTRY

The Conference of the new *Iskra*-ists did not keep to the anarchist position into which the new *Iskra* had talked itself (only "from below," not "from below and from above"). The absurdity of admitting the possibility of an insurrection and not admitting the possibility of victory and participation in a provisional revolutionary government was too glaring. The resolution therefore introduced certain reservations and restrictions into the solution of the question proposed by Martynov and Martov. Let us consider these reservations as stated in the following section of the resolution:

"These tactics" ("to remain the party of extreme revolutionary opposition") "do not, of course, in any way exclude the expediency of a partial and episodic seizure of power and the establishment of revolutionary communes in one or another city, in one or another district, exclusively for the purpose of helping to spread the insurrection and of disrupting the government."

That being the case, it means that in principle they admit the possibility of action not only from below, but also from above. It means that the proposition laid down in L. Martov's well-known article in the *Iskra* (No. 93) is discarded, and that the tactics of *Vperyod*, i.e., not only "from below," but also "from above," are acknowledged as correct.

Further, the seizure of power (even if partial, episodic, etc.) obviously presupposes the participation not only of Social-Democrats and not only of the proletariat. This follows from the fact that it is not only the proletariat that is interested and takes an active part in a democratic revolution. This follows from the fact that the insurrection is a "popular" one, as is stated in the beginning of the resolution we are discussing, that "non-proletarian groups" (the words used in the Conference resolution on the uprising), i.e., the bourgeoisie, also take part in it. Hence, the principle that any participation of Socialists in a provisional revolutionary government jointly with the petty bourgeoisie is treachery to the working class *was thrown overboard by the Conference,* which is what the *Vperyod*[31] sought to achieve. "Treachery" does not cease to be treachery because the action which constitutes it is partial, episodic, local, etc. Hence, the parallel drawn between the participation in a provisional revolutionary government and vulgar Jaurèsism *was thrown overboard* by the Conference, which is what the *Vperyod* sought to achieve. A government does not cease to be a government because its power does not extend to many cities but is confined to a single city, does not extend to many districts but is confined to a single district; nor because of the name that is given to it. Thus, *the formulation of the principles of this question* which the new *Iskra* tried to give *was discarded by the Conference.*

Let us see whether the restrictions imposed by the Conference on the formation of revolutionary governments and participation in them, which is now admitted in principle, are reasonable. What difference there is between the concept "episodic" and the concept "provisional," we do not know. We are afraid that this "new" and foreign word is merely a screen for lack of clear thinking. It *seems* "more profound," but actually it is only more obscure and confused. What is the difference between the "expediency" of a partial "seizure of power" in a city or district, and participation in a provisional revolutionary government of the entire state? Do not "cities" include a city like St. Petersburg, where the events of January 9 took place? Do not districts include the Caucasus, which is bigger than many a state? Will not the problems (which at one time vexed the new *Iskra*) of what to do with the prisons, the police, public funds, etc., confront us the moment we "seize power" in a single city, let alone in a district? No one will deny, of course, that if we lack sufficient forces, if the insurrection is not wholly successful, or if the victory is indecisive, it is possible that provisional revolutionary governments will be set up in separate localities, in individual cities and the like. But what is the point of such an assumption, gentlemen? Do not you yourselves speak in the beginning of the resolution about a "decisive victory of the revolution," about a "victorious popular insurrection"?? Since when have the Social-Democrats taken over the job of the anarchists: to divide the attention and the aims of the proletariat, to direct its attention to the "partial" instead of the general, the single, the integral and complete? While presupposing the "seizure of power" in a city, you yourselves speak of "spreading the insurrection" — to another city, may we venture to think?

to all cities, may we dare to hope? Your conclusions, gentlemen, are as unsound and haphazard, as contradictory and confused as your premises. The Third Congress of the R.S.D.L.P. gave an exhaustive and clear answer to the question of a provisional revolutionary government in general. And this answer covers all cases of local provisional governments as well. The answer given by the Conference, however, by artificially and arbitrarily singling out a *part* of the question, merely *evades* (but unsuccessfully) the issue as a whole, and creates confusion.

What does the term "revolutionary communes" mean? Does it differ from the term "provisional revolutionary government," and, if so, in what respect? The Conference gentlemen themselves do not know. Confusion of revolutionary thought leads them, as very often happens, to *revolutionary phrasemongering.* Yes, the use of the words "revolutionary commune" in a resolution passed by representatives of Social-Democracy is revolutionary phrasemongering and nothing else. Marx more than once condemned such phrasemongering, when "fascinating" terms of the *bygone past* were used to hide the tasks of the future. In such cases a fascinating term that has played its part in history becomes futile and pernicious trumpery, a child's rattle. We must give the workers and the whole people a clear and unambiguous explanation as to *why* we want a provisional revolutionary government to be set up, and *exactly what changes* we shall accomplish, if we exercise decisive influence on the government, on the very morrow of the victory of the popular insurrection which has already commenced. These are the questions that confront political leaders.

The Third Congress of the R.S.D.L.P. gave perfectly clear answers to these questions and drew up a complete program of these changes — the minimum program of our Party. The word "commune," however, is not an answer at all; it only serves to confuse people by the distant echo of a sonorous phrase, or empty rhetoric. The more we cherish the memory of the Paris Commune of 1871, for instance, the less permissible is it to refer to it offhand, without analyzing its mistakes and the special conditions attending it. To do so would be to follow the absurd example of the Blanquists — whom Engels ridiculed — who (in 1874, in their "Manifesto") paid homage to every act of the Commune.[32] What reply will a "Conferencer" give to a worker who asks him about *this* "revolutionary commune" that is mentioned in the resolution? He will only be able to tell him that this is the name, known in history, of a workers' government that was unable to, and could not at that time, distinguish between the elements of a democratic revolution and those of a socialist revolution, that confused the tasks of fighting for a republic with the tasks of fighting for Socialism, that was unable to carry out the task of launching an energetic military offensive against Versailles, that made a mistake in not seizing the Bank of France, etc. In short, whether in your answer you refer to the Paris Commune or to some other commune, your answer will be: it was a government *such as ours should not be*. A fine answer, indeed! Does it not testify to pedantic moralizing and impotence on the part of a revolutionary who says nothing about the practical program of the Party and inappropriately begins to give lessons in history in a resolution? Does this not reveal the very mistake which they unsuccessfully accuse us of having committed, i.e., of confusing a democratic revolution with a socialist revolution, between which none of the "communes" differentiated?

The aim of a provisional government (so inappropriately termed "commune") is declared to be "exclusively" to spread the insurrection and to disrupt the government. Taken in its literal sense, the word "exclusively" eliminates all other aims; it is an echo of the absurd theory of "only from below." Such elimination of other aims is another instance of shortsightedness and lack of reflection. A "revolutionary commune," i.e., a revolutionary government, even if only in a single city, will inevitably have to administer (even if provisionally, "partly, episodically") *all* the affairs of state, and it is the height of folly to hide one's head under one's wing and refuse to see this. This government will have to enact an eight-hour working day, establish workers' inspection of factories, institute free universal education, introduce the election of judges, set up peasant committees, etc.; in a word, it will certainly have to carry out a number of reforms. To designate these reforms as "helping to spread the insurrection" would be playing with words and deliberately causing greater confusion in a matter which requires absolute clarity.

The concluding part of the new *Iskra*-ists' resolution does not provide any new material for a criticism of the trends of principles of "Economism" which has revived in our Party, but it illustrates what has been said above from a somewhat different angle.

Here is that part:

"Only in one event should Social-Democracy, on its own initiative, direct its efforts towards seizing power and holding it as long as possible — namely, in the event of the revolution spreading to the advanced countries of Western Europe, where conditions for the achievement of Socialism have already reached a certain"(?) "degree of maturity. In that event the limited historical scope of the Russian revolution can be considerably widened and the possibility of entering the path of socialist reforms will arise.

"By framing its tactics in accordance with the view that, during the whole period of the revolution, the Social-Democratic Party will retain the position of extreme revolutionary opposition to all the governments that may succeed one another in the course of the revolution, Social-Democracy will best be able to prepare itself to utilize governmental power if it falls"(??) "into its hands."

The basic idea here is the one that the *Vperyod* has repeatedly formulated, stating that we must not be afraid (as is Martynov) of a complete victory for Social-Democracy in a democratic revolution, i.e., of a revolutionary-democratic dictatorship of the proletariat and the peasantry, for such a victory will enable us to rouse Europe, and the socialist proletariat of Europe, after throwing off the yoke of the bourgeoisie, will in its turn help us to accomplish the socialist revolution. But see how this idea is worsened in the new *Iskra*-ists' rendering of it. We shall not dwell on details — on the absurd assumption that power could "fall" into the hands of a class-conscious party which considers seizure of power harmful tactics; on the fact that in Europe the conditions for Socialism have reached not a certain degree of maturity, but are already mature; on the fact that our Party program does not speak of socialist changes at all, but only of a socialist revolution. Let us take the principal and basic difference between the idea presented by the *Vperyod* and that presented in the resolution. The *Vperyod* set the revolutionary proletariat of Russia an active aim: to win the battle for democracy and to use this victory for carrying the revolution into Europe. The resolution fails to grasp this connection between our "decisive victory" (not in the new *Iskra* sense) and the revolution in Europe, and therefore it speaks not about the tasks of the proletariat, not about the prospects of *its* victory, but about one of the possibilities in general: "in the event of the revolution spreading. . . ." The *Vperyod* pointedly and definitely indicated — and this was incorporated in the resolution of the Third Congress of the Russian Social-Democratic Labour Party — how "governmental power" can and must "be utilized" in the interests of the proletariat, bearing in mind what can be achieved immediately, at the given stage of social development, and what must first be achieved as a democratic prerequisite of the struggle for Socialism. Here, also, the resolution hopelessly drags at the tail when it states: "will be able to prepare itself to utilize," but fails to say *how* it will be able, *how* it will prepare itself, and to utilize *for what*? We have no doubt, for instance, that the new *Iskra*-ists may be "able to prepare themselves to utilize" the leading position in the Party; but the point is that the way they have utilized, their preparation up till now, do not hold out much hope of possibility being transformed into reality. . . .

The *Vperyod* quite definitely stated wherein lies the real "possibility of holding power" — namely, in the revolutionary-democratic dictatorship of the proletariat and the peasantry, in their joint mass strength, which is capable of outweighing all the forces of counterrevolution, in the inevitable concurrence of their interests in *democratic* changes. Here, too, the resolution of the Conference gives us nothing positive, it merely evades the question. Surely, the possibility of holding power in Russia must be determined by the composition of the social forces in Russia itself, by the circumstances of the democratic revolution which is now taking place in our country. A victory of the proletariat in Europe (it is still somewhat of a far cry between carrying the revolution into Europe and the victory of the proletariat) will give rise to a desperate counter-revolutionary struggle on the part of the Russian bourgeoisie — yet the resolution of the new *Iskra*-ists does not say a word about this counterrevolutionary force, the importance of which has been appraised in the resolution of the Third Congress of the R.S.D.L.P. If in our fight for a republic and democracy we could not rely upon the peasantry as well as on the proletariat, the prospect of our "holding power" would be hopeless. But if it is not hopeless, if a "decisive victory of the revolution over tsarism" opens up such a possibility, then we must point to it, we must actively call for its transformation into reality and issue practical slogans not only *for the contingency* of the revolution being carried into Europe, but also *for the purpose* of carrying it there. The reference made by the *khvostist* Social-Democrats to the "limited historical scope of the Russian revolution" merely serves to cover up their limited understanding of the aims of this democratic revolution and of the leading role of the proletariat in this revolution!

One of the objections raised to the slogan of "the revolutionary-democratic dictatorship of the proletariat and the peasantry" is that dictatorship presupposes a "single will" (*Iskra*, No. 95), and that there can be no single will of the proletariat and the petty bourgeoisie. This objection is unsound, for it is based on an abstract, "metaphysical" interpretation of the term "single will." There can be a single will in one respect and not a single will in another. The absence of unity on questions of Socialism and in the struggle for Socialism does not preclude singleness of will on questions of democracy and in the struggle for a republic. To forget this would be tantamount to forgetting the logical and historical difference between a democratic and a socialist revolution. To forget this would be tantamount to forgetting the character of the democratic revolution as a revolution *of the whole people*: if it is "of the whole people" it means that there *is* "singleness of will" precisely in so far as this revolution satisfies the common needs and requirements of the whole people. Beyond the bounds of democracy there can be no question of the proletariat and the peasant bourgeoisie having a single will. Class struggle between them is inevitable; but it is in a democratic republic that this struggle will be the most thoroughgoing and widespread struggle of the people *for Socialism*. Like everything else in the world, the revolutionary-democratic dictatorship of the proletariat and the peasantry has a past and a future. Its past is autocracy, serfdom, monarchy and privilege. In the struggle against this past, in the struggle against counterrevolution, a "single will" of the proletariat and the peasantry is possible, for here there is unity of interests.

Its future is the struggle against private property, the struggle of the wage worker against the employer, the struggle for Socialism. Here singleness of will is impossible.* Here our path lies not from autocracy to a republic but from a petty-bourgeois democratic republic to Socialism.

Of course, in actual historical circumstances, the elements of the past become interwoven with those of the future, the two paths cross. Wage labour, with its struggle against private property, exists under the autocracy as well; it is generated even under serfdom. But this does not in the least prevent us from drawing a logical and historical dividing line between the major stages of development. We all draw a distinction between bourgeois revolution and socialist revolution, we all absolutely insist on the necessity of drawing a most strict line between them; but can it be denied that individual, particular elements of the two revolutions become interwoven in history? Have there not been a number of socialist movements and attempts at establishing Socialism in the period of democratic revolutions in Europe? And will not the future socialist revolution in Europe still have to do a very great deal that has been left undone in the field of democracy?

A Social-Democrat must never for a moment forget that the proletariat will inevitably have to wage the class struggle for Socialism even against the most democratic and republican bourgeoisie and petty bourgeoisie. This is beyond doubt. Hence the absolute necessity of a separate, independent, strictly class party of Social-Democracy. Hence the temporary nature of our tactics of "striking jointly" with the bourgeoisie and the duty of keeping a strict watch "over our ally, as over an enemy," etc. All this is also beyond the

---

* The development of capitalism, which is more widespread and rapid where there is freedom, will inevitably put a speedy end to singleness of will; the sooner counterrevolution and reaction are crushed, the sooner will the singleness of will come to an end.

slightest doubt. But it would be ridiculous and reactionary to deduce from this that we must forget, ignore or neglect these tasks which, although transient and temporary, are vital at the present time. The fight against the autocracy is a temporary and transient task of the Socialists, but to ignore or neglect this task in any way would be tantamount to betraying Socialism and rendering a service to reaction. The revolutionary-democratic dictatorship of the proletariat and the peasantry is unquestionably only a transient, temporary aim of the Socialists, but to ignore this aim in the period of a democratic revolution would be downright reactionary.

Concrete political aims must be set in concrete circumstances. All things are relative, all things flow and all things change. The program of the German Social-Democratic Party does not contain the demand for a republic. The situation in Germany is such that this question can in practice hardly be separated from the question of Socialism (although even as regards Germany, Engels, in his comments on the draft of the Erfurt Program in 1891, warned against belittling the importance of a republic and of the struggle for a republic!).[33] In the Russian Social-Democratic Party the question of eliminating the demand for a republic from its program and agitation has never even arisen, for in our country there can be no talk of an indissoluble connection between the question of a republic and the question of Socialism. It was quite natural for a German Social-Democrat of 1898 not to put the special question of a republic in the forefront, and this evokes neither surprise nor condemnation. But a German Social-Democrat who in 1848 would have left the question of a republic in the shade would have been a downright traitor to the revolution. There is no such thing as abstract truth. Truth is always concrete.

The time will come when the struggle against the Russian autocracy will end and the period of democratic revolution will be over in Russia; then it will be ridiculous to talk about "singleness of will" of the proletariat and the peasantry, about a democratic dictatorship, etc. When that time comes we shall attend directly to the question of the socialist dictatorship of the proletariat and deal with it at greater length. But at present the party of the advanced class cannot but strive most energetically for a decisive victory of the democratic revolution over tsarism. And a decisive victory means nothing else than the revolutionary-democratic dictatorship of the proletariat and the peasantry.

*N O T E*[34]

1) We would remind the reader that in the polemics between the *Iskra* and the *Vperyod*, the former referred among other things to Engels' letter to Turati, in which Engels warned the (future) leader of the Italian reformists not to confuse the democratic with the socialist revolution.[35] The impending revolution in Italy — wrote Engels about the political situation in Italy in 1894 — will be a petty-bourgeois, democratic and not a socialist revolution. The *Iskra* reproached the *Vperyod* with having departed from the principle laid down by Engels. This reproach was unjustified, because the *Vperyod* (No. 14)[36] fully acknowledged, on the whole, the correctness of Marx's theory of the difference between the three main forces in the revolutions of the nineteenth century. According to this theory, the following forces take a stand against the old order, against the autoc-

racy, feudalism, serfdom: 1) the liberal big bourgeoisie, 2) the radical petty bourgeoisie, 3) the proletariat. The first fights for nothing more than a constitutional monarchy; the second, for a democratic republic; the third, for a socialist revolution. To confuse the petty-bourgeois struggle for a complete democratic revolution with the proletarian struggle for a socialist revolution spells political bankruptcy for a Socialist. Marx's warning to this effect is quite justified. But it is precisely for this very reason that the slogan "revolutionary communes" is erroneous, because the very mistake committed by the communes that have existed in history is that they confused the democratic revolution with the socialist revolution. On the other hand, our slogan — a revolutionary democratic dictatorship of the proletariat and the peasantry — fully safeguards us against this mistake. While recognizing the incontestably bourgeois nature of the revolution, which is incapable of *directly* overstepping the bounds of a mere democratic revolution, our slogan *pushes forward* this particular revolution and strives to mould it into forms most advantageous to the proletariat; consequently, it strives to make the very most of the democratic revolution in order to attain the greatest success in the further struggle of the proletariat for Socialism.

## 11. A CURSORY COMPARISON BETWEEN SEVERAL OF THE RESOLUTIONS OF THE THIRD CONGRESS OF THE R.S.D.L.P. AND THOSE OF THE "CONFERENCE"

The question of the provisional revolutionary government is the pivot of the tactical questions of the Social-

Democratic movement at the present time. It is neither possible nor necessary to dwell in as great detail on the other resolutions of the Conference. We shall confine ourselves merely to indicating briefly a few points which confirm the difference in principle, analyzed above, between the tactical trends of the resolutions of the Third Congress of the R.S.D.L.P. and those of the Conference resolutions.

Take the question of the attitude towards the tactics of the government on the eve of the revolution. Once again you will find a comprehensive answer to this question in one of the resolutions of the Third Congress of the R.S.D.L.P. This resolution takes into consideration all the multifarious conditions and tasks of the particular moment: the exposure of the hypocrisy of the government's concessions, the utilization of "travesties of popular representation," the achievement by revolutionary means of the urgent demands of the working class (the principal one being the eight-hour working day), and, finally, resistance to the Black Hundreds. In the Conference resolutions this question is scattered over several sections: "resistance to the dark forces of reaction" is mentioned only in the preamble of the resolution on the attitude to other parties. Participation in elections to representative bodies is considered separately from the question of "compromises" between tsarism and the bourgeoisie. Instead of calling for the achievement of an eight-hour working day by revolutionary means, a special resolution, with the high-sounding title "On the Economic Struggle," merely repeats (after high-flown and very stupid phrases about "the central place occupied by the labour question in the public life of Russia") the old slogan of agitation for "the legislative institution of an eight-hour working day." The inadequacy and the belatedness of this slogan at the present time are too obvious to require proof.

The question of open political action. The Third Congress takes into consideration the impending *radical* change in our activity. Secret activity and the development of the secret apparatus must on no account be abandoned: this would be playing into the hands of the police and be of the utmost advantage to the government. But at the same time we cannot start too soon thinking about open action as well. Expedient forms of such action and, consequently, special apparatus — less secret — must be *prepared* immediately for this purpose. The legal and semilegal societies must be made use of with a view to transforming them, as far as possible, into bases of the future open Social-Democratic Labour Party in Russia.

Here too the Conference divides up the question, and fails to issue any integral slogans. There bobs up as a separate point the ridiculous instruction to the Organization Commission to see to the "placing" of its legally functioning publicists. There is the wholly absurd decision "to subordinate to its influence the democratic newspapers that set themselves the aim of rendering assistance to the working-class movement." This is the professed aim of all our legal liberal newspapers, nearly all of which are of the *Osvobozhdeniye* trend. Why should not the editors of the *Iskra* make a start themselves in carrying out their advice and give us an example of how to subject the *Osvobozhdeniye* to Social-Democratic influence? ... Instead of the slogan of utilizing the legally existing unions for the purpose of establishing bases for the *Party*, we are given, first, particular advice about the "trade" unions only (that all Party members must join them) and, secondly, advice to guide "the revolutionary organizations of the workers"="organizations not officially constituted" = "revolutionary workers' clubs." How these "clubs" come to be classed as unofficially constituted organizations, what these "clubs" really are — goodness only knows. Instead of definite and clear instructions from a supreme Party body, we have some jottings of ideas and the rough drafts of publicists. We get no complete picture of the beginning of the Party's transition to an entirely new basis in all its work.

The "peasant question" was presented by the Party Congress and by the Conference in entirely different ways. The Congress drew up a resolution on the "attitude to the peasant movement," the Conference on "work among the peasants." In the one case prime importance is attached to the task of guiding the widespread revolutionary-democratic movement in the general national interests of the fight against tsarism. In the other instance, the question is reduced to mere "work" among a particular section of society. In the one case, a central practical slogan for our agitation is advanced, calling for the immediate organization of revolutionary peasant committees in order to carry out all the democratic changes. In the other, a "demand for the organization of committees" is to be presented to a constituent assembly. Why must we wait for this constituent assembly? Will it really be constituent? Will it be stable without the preliminary and simultaneous establishment of revolutionary peasant committees? All these questions are ignored by the Conference. All its decisions reflect the general idea which we have traced — namely, that in the bourgeois revolution we must do only our special work, without setting ourselves the aim of leading the entire democratic movement and of doing this independently. Just as the Economists constantly harped on the idea that the Social-Democrats should concern themselves with the economic struggle, leaving it to the liberals to take care of the political struggle, so the new *Iskra*-ists keep harping in all their discussions on the idea that we should creep into a modest corner out of the way of the bourgeois revolution, leaving it to the bourgeoisie to do the active work of carrying out the revolution.

Finally, we cannot but note also the resolution on the attitude towards other parties. The resolution of the Third Congress of the R.S.D.L.P. speaks of exposing all the limitations and inadequacies of the bourgeois movement for emancipation, without entertaining the naive idea of enumerating every possible instance of such limitation from congress to congress or of drawing a line of distinction between bad bourgeois and good bourgeois. The Conference, repeating the mistake made by Starover, persistently searched for such a line, developed the famous "litmus paper" theory. Starover started from a very good idea: to put the strictest possible terms to the bourgeoisie. Only he forgot that any attempt to separate in advance the bourgeois democrats who are worthy of approval, agreements, etc., from those who are unworthy leads to a "formula" which is immediately thrown overboard by the development of events and which introduces confusion into the proletarian class consciousness. The emphasis is shifted from real unity in the struggle to declarations, promises, slogans. Starover was of the opinion that "universal and equal suffrage, direct elections and secret ballot" was such a radical slogan. But before two years elapsed the "litmus paper" proved its worthlessness, the slogan of universal suffrage was taken over by the *Osvobozhdentsi,* who not only came no closer to Social-

Democracy as a result of this, but, on the contrary, tried by means of this very slogan to mislead the workers and divert them from Socialism.

Now the new *Iskra*-ists are setting "terms" that are even "stricter," they are "demanding" from the enemies of tsarism "energetic and unequivocal" (!?) "support of every determined action of the organized proletariat," etc., up to and including "active participation in the self-armament of the people." The line has been drawn much further — but nonetheless this line is *again already obsolete,* it revealed its worthlessness at once. Why, for instance, is there no slogan of a republic? How is it that the Social-Democrats — in the interest of "relentless revolutionary war against all the foundations of the system of social estates and the monarchy" — "demand" from the bourgeois democrats anything you like except a fight for a republic?

That this question is not mere captiousness, that the mistake of the new *Iskra*-ists is of most vital political significance is proved by the "Russian Liberation League" (see *Proletary,* No. 4).* These "enemies of tsarism" will fully meet all the "requirements" of the new *Iskra*-ists. And yet we have shown that the spirit of *Osvobozhdeniye* reigns in the program (or lack of program) of this "Russian Liberation

---

* *Proletary,* No. 4, which appeared on June 4, 1905, contained a lengthy article entitled "A New Revolutionary Labour League" (see Lenin, *Collected Works,* 4th Russ. ed., Vol. VIII, pp. 465-76. — *Ed.*). The article gives the contents of the appeals issued by this league which assumed the name of "Russian Liberation League" and which set itself the aim of convening a constituent assembly with the aid of an armed insurrection. Further, the article defines the attitude of the Social-Democrats to such non-Party leagues. How far this league really existed, and what its fate was in the revolution is absolutely unknown to us. [Author's note to the 1907 edition.]

League" and that the *Osvobozhdentsi* can easily take it in tow. The Conference, however, declares in the concluding section of the resolution that "Social-Democracy will continue to oppose the *hypocritical friends of the people*, all those political parties which, though they display a liberal and democratic banner, refuse to render genuine support to the revolutionary struggle of the proletariat." The "Russian Liberation League" not only does not refuse this support but offers it most insistently. Is that a guarantee that the leaders of this League are not "hypocritical friends of the people," even though they are *Osvobozhdentsi*?

You see: by inventing "terms" in advance and presenting "demands" which are ludicrous by reason of their grim impotence, the new *Iskra*-ists immediately put themselves in a ridiculous position. Their terms and demands immediately prove inadequate when it comes to gauging living realities. Their chase after formulae is hopeless, for no formula can embrace all the various manifestations of hypocrisy, inconsistency and limitations of the bourgeois democrats. It is not a matter of "litmus paper," of forms, or written and printed demands, nor is it a matter of drawing, in advance, a line of distinction between hypocritical and sincere "friends of the people"; it is a matter of real unity in the struggle, of unabating criticism by Social-Democrats of every "uncertain" step taken by bourgeois democracy. What is needed for a "genuine consolidation of all the social forces interested in democratic change" is not the "points" over which the Conference laboured so assiduously and so vainly, but the ability to put forward genuinely revolutionary slogans. For this slogans are needed that will raise the revolutionary and republican bourgeoisie to the level of the proletariat and not reduce the aims of the proletariat to the level of the monarchist bourgeoisie. For this the most energetic participation in the insurrection and not sophist evasions of the urgent task of armed insurrection is needed.

## 12. WILL THE SWEEP OF THE DEMOCRATIC REVOLUTION BE DIMINISHED IF THE BOURGEOISIE RECOILS FROM IT?

The foregoing lines were already written when we received a copy of the resolutions adopted by the Caucasian Conference of the new *Iskra*-ists, published by the *Iskra*. Better material than this pour la bonne bouche (for dessert) we could not even have invented.

The editors of the *Iskra* quite justly remark: "On the fundamental question of tactics, the Caucasian Conference also arrived at a decision *analogous*" (in truth!) "to the one adopted by the All-Russian Conference" (i.e., of the new *Iskra*-ists). "The question of the attitude of Social-Democracy towards a provisional revolutionary government has been settled by the Caucasian comrades in the spirit of most outspoken opposition to the new method advocated by the *Vperyod* group and by the delegates of the so-called Congress who joined it." "It must be admitted that the formulation of the tactics of the proletarian party in a bourgeois revolution as given by the Conference is *very apt*."

What is true is true. No one could have given a more "apt" formulation of the fundamental error of the new *Iskra*-ists. We shall quote this formulation in full, indicating in parentheses first the blossoms and then the fruit presented at the end.

Here is the resolution of the Caucasian Conference of new *Iskra*-ists on a provisional revolutionary government:

"Whereas we consider it to be our task to take advantage of the revolutionary situation to render more profound" (of course! They should have added: "à la Martynov!") "the Social-Democratic consciousness of the proletariat" (only to render the consciousness more profound, and not to win a republic? What a "profound" conception of revolution!) "and in order to secure for the Party fullest freedom to criticize the nascent bourgeois-state system" (it is not our business to secure a republic! Our business is only to secure freedom of criticism. Anarchist ideas give rise to anarchist language: "bourgeois-state" system!), "the Conference declares against the formation of a Social-Democratic provisional government and joining such a government" (recall the resolution passed by the Bakuninists ten months before the Spanish revolution and referred to by Engels: see the *Proletary*, No. 3),[37] "and considers it to be the most expedient course to exercise pressure from without" (from below and not from above) "upon the bourgeois provisional government in order to secure a feasible measure" (?!) "of democratization of the state system. The Conference believes that the formation of a provisional government by Social-Democrats, or their joining such a government, would lead, on the one hand, to the masses of the proletariat becoming disappointed in the Social-Democratic Party and abandoning it because the Social-Democrats, in spite of the fact that they had seized power, would not be able to satisfy the pressing needs of the working class, including the establishment of Socialism" (a republic is not a pressing need! The authors, in their innocence, do not notice that they are speaking a purely anarchist language, as if they were repudiating participation in bourgeois revolutions!), "and, on the other hand, *will cause the bourgeois classes to recoil from the revolution and thus diminish its sweep.*"

That is where the trouble lies. That is where anarchist ideas become interwoven (as is constantly the case among the West-European Bernsteinians also) with the purest opportunism. Just think of it: not to join a provisional government because this will cause the bourgeoisie to recoil from the revolution and thus diminish the sweep of the revolution! Here, indeed, we have the new *Iskra* philosophy in its complete, pure and consistent form: the revolution is a bourgeois revolution, therefore we must bow down to bourgeois philistinism and make way for it. If we are guided, even in part, even for a moment, by the consideration that our participation may cause the bourgeoisie to recoil, we thereby simply yield leadership in the revolution entirely to the bourgeois classes. We thereby place the proletariat entirely under the tutelage of the bourgeoisie (while retaining complete "freedom of criticism"!!), compelling the proletariat to be meek and mild so as not to cause the bourgeoisie to recoil. We emasculate the most vital needs of the proletariat, namely, its political needs — which the Economists and their epigones have never properly understood — so as not to cause the bourgeoisie to recoil. We completely abandon the field of revolutionary struggle for the achievement of democracy to the extent required by the proletariat for the field of bargaining with the bourgeoisie, betraying our principles, betraying the revolution to purchase the bourgeoisie's voluntary consent ("that it might not recoil").

In two brief lines, the Caucasian new *Iskra*-ists managed to express the quintessence of the tactics of betrayal of the revolution and of converting the proletariat into a wretched appendage of the bourgeois classes. The tendency, which we traced above to the mistakes of the new *Iskra*-ists, now stands out before us as a clear and definite principle, viz., to drag at the tail of the monarchist bourgeoisie. Since the establishment of a republic would cause (and is already causing: Mr. Struve, for example) the bourgeoisie to recoil, therefore, down with the fight for a republic. Since every resolute and consistent democratic demand of the proletariat always and everywhere in the world causes the bourgeoisie to recoil, therefore, hide in your lairs, comrades and fellow workers, act only from without, do not dream of using the instruments and weapons of the "bourgeois-state" system in the interests of the revolution, and reserve for yourselves "freedom to criticize"!

Here the fundamental fallacy of their very conception of the term "bourgeois revolution" has come to the surface. The Martynov or new *Iskra* "conception" of this term leads straight to a betrayal of the cause of the proletariat to the bourgeoisie.

Those who have forgotten the old Economism, those who do not study it or remember it, will find it difficult to understand the present echo of Economism. Recall the Bernsteinian *Credo*.[38] From "purely proletarian" views and programs, people arrived at the conclusion: we, the Social-Democrats, must concern ourselves with economics, with the real cause of labour, with freedom to criticize all political chicanery, with rendering Social-Democratic work really more profound. Politics are for the liberals. God save us from dropping into "revolutionism": that will cause the bourgeoisie to recoil. Those who read the whole *Credo* over again or the Supplement to No. 9 of the *Rabochaya Mysl*[39] (September 1899) will be able to follow this entire line of reasoning.

Today we have the same thing, only on a large scale, applied to an appraisal of the whole of the "great" Russian revolution — alas, already vulgarized and reduced to a travesty in advance by the theoreticians of orthodox philistinism! We, the Social-Democrats, must concern ourselves with freedom of criticism, with rendering class consciousness more profound, with action from without. They, the bourgeois classes, must have freedom to act, a free field for revolutionary (read: liberal) leadership, freedom to put through "reforms" from above.

These vulgarizers of Marxism have never pondered over what Marx said about the need of substituting the criticism of weapons for the weapon of criticism.[40] Taking the name of Marx in vain, they, in actual fact, draw up resolutions on tactics wholly in the spirit of the Frankfurt bourgeois windbags, who freely criticized absolutism and rendered democratic consciousness more profound, but failed to understand that the time of revolution is the time of action, of action both from above and from below. Having converted Marxism into pedantry, they have made the ideology of the advanced, most determined and energetic revolutionary class the ideology of its most undeveloped strata, which shrink from the difficult revolutionary-democratic tasks and leave it to Messrs. the Struves to take care of these democratic tasks.

If the bourgeois classes recoil from the revolution because the Social-Democrats join the revolutionary government, they will thereby "diminish the sweep" of the revolution.

Listen to this, Russian workers: The sweep of the revolution will be mightier if it is carried out by Messrs. the

Struves, who are not frightened away by the Social-Democrats and who want, not victory over tsarism, but to come to terms with it. The sweep of the revolution will be mightier if, of the two possible outcomes which we have outlined above, the first eventuates, i.e., if the monarchist bourgeoisie comes to terms with the autocracy concerning a "constitution" à la Shipov!

Social-Democrats who write such disgraceful things in resolutions intended for the guidance of the whole Party, or who approve of such "apt" resolutions, are so blinded by their pedantry, which has utterly eroded the living spirit out of Marxism, that they do not see how these resolutions convert all their other fine words into mere phrasemongering. Take any of their articles in the *Iskra,* or take even the notorious pamphlet written by our celebrated Martynov — you will read there about a *popular* insurrection, about carrying the revolution to *completion,* about striving to rely upon the *common people* in the fight against the inconsistent bourgeoisie. But then all these excellent things become miserable phrasemongering immediately you accept or approve of the idea that "the sweep of the revolution" will be "diminished" as a consequence of the alienation of the bourgeoisie. One of two things, gentlemen: either we, together with the people, must strive to carry out the revolution and win a complete victory over tsarism *in spite of* the inconsistent, self-seeking and cowardly bourgeoisie, or we do not accept this "in spite of," we fear lest the bourgeoisie "recoil" from the revolution, in which case we betray the proletariat and the people to the bourgeoisie — to the inconsistent, self-seeking and cowardly bourgeoisie.

Don't try to misinterpret what I have said. Don't start howling that you are being accused of deliberate treachery.

No, you have always been crawling and have at last crawled into the mire as unconsciously as the Economists of old, drawn inexorably and irrevocably down the inclined plane of making Marxism "more profound" to antirevolutionary, soulless and lifeless "philosophizing."

Have you ever considered, gentlemen, what real social forces determine "the sweep of the revolution"? Let us leave aside the forces of foreign politics, of international combinations, which have turned out very favourably for us at the present time, but which we all leave out of our discussion, and rightly so, inasmuch as we are concerned with the question of the internal forces of Russia. Look at these internal social forces. Aligned against the revolution are the autocracy, the imperial court, the police, the bureaucracy, the army and the handful of high nobility. The deeper the indignation of the people grows, the less reliable become the troops, and the more the bureaucracy wavers. Moreover, the bourgeoisie, on the whole, is now in favour of the revolution, is zealously making speeches about liberty, holding forth more and more frequently in the name of the people, and even in the name of the revolution.* But we Marxists all know from theory and from daily and hourly observation of our liberals, Zemstvo-ists and *Osvobozhdentsi* that the bourgeoisie is inconsistent, self-seeking and cowardly in its support of the revolution. The bourgeoisie, in the mass, will inevitably turn towards counterrevolution, towards the autocracy, against the revolution and against the people, immediately its narrow, selfish interests are met, immediately it "recoils" from consistent democracy (*and it is already*

---

* Of interest in this connection is Mr. Struve's open letter to Jaurès, recently published by the latter in *L'Humanité*[41] and by Mr. Struve in the *Osvobozhdeniye*, No. 72.

*recoiling from it!*). There remains the "people," that is, the proletariat and the peasantry: the proletariat alone can be relied on to march to the end, for it is going far beyond the democratic revolution. That is why the proletariat fights in the front ranks for a republic and contemptuously rejects silly and unworthy advice to take care not to frighten away the bourgeoisie. The peasantry includes a great number of semiproletarian as well as petty-bourgeois elements. This causes it also to be unstable and compels the proletariat to unite in a strictly class party. But the instability of the peasantry differs radically from the instability of the bourgeoisie, for at the present time the peasantry is interested not so much in the absolute preservation of private property as in the confiscation of the landed estates, one of the principal forms of private property. While this does not make the peasantry become socialist or cease to be petty-bourgeois, it is capable of becoming a wholehearted and most radical adherent of the democratic revolution. The peasantry will inevitably become such if only the progress of revolutionary events, which is enlightening it, is not checked too soon by the treachery of the bourgeoisie and the defeat of the proletariat. Subject to this condition, the peasantry will inevitably become a bulwark of the revolution and the republic, for only a completely victorious revolution can give the peasantry *everything* in the sphere of agrarian reforms — *everything* that the peasants desire, of which they dream, and of which they truly stand in need (not for the abolition of capitalism as the "Socialist-Revolutionaries" imagine, but) in order to emerge from the mire of semiserfdom, from the gloom of oppression and servitude, in order to improve their living conditions as much as it is possible to improve them under the system of commodity production.

Moreover, the peasantry is attached to the revolution not only by the prospect of radical agrarian reform but by its general and permanent interests. Even in fighting the proletariat the peasantry stands in need of democracy, for only a democratic system is capable of giving exact expression to its interests and of ensuring its predominance as the mass, as the majority. The more enlightened the peasantry becomes (and since the war with Japan it is becoming enlightened much more rapidly than those who are accustomed to measure enlightenment by the school standard suspect), the more consistently and determinedly will it favour a thoroughgoing democratic revolution; for, unlike the bourgeoisie, it has nothing to fear from the supremacy of the people, but, on the contrary, stands to gain by it. A democratic republic will become the ideal of the peasantry as soon as it begins to free itself from its naive monarchism, because the enlightened monarchism of the bourgeois stock-jobbers (with an upper chamber, etc.) implies for the peasantry the same disfranchisement and the same downtroddenness and ignorance as it suffers from today, only slightly glossed over with the varnish of European constitutionalism.

That is why the bourgeoisie as a class naturally and inevitably strives to come under the wing of the liberal-monarchist party, while the peasantry, in the mass, strives to come under the leadership of the revolutionary and republican party. That is why the bourgeoisie is incapable of carrying the democratic revolution to its consummation, while the peasantry is capable of doing so, and we must exert all our efforts to help it to do so.

It may be objected: but this requires no proof, this is all ABC; all Social-Democrats understand this perfectly well. But that is not so. It is not understood by those who can talk about "the sweep" of the revolution being "diminished" because the bourgeoisie will fall away from it. Such people repeat the words of our agrarian program that they have learned by rote without understanding their meaning, for otherwise they would not be frightened by the concept of the revolutionary-democratic dictatorship of the proletariat and the peasantry, which inevitably follows from the entire Marxian world outlook and from our program; otherwise they would not restrict the sweep of the great Russian revolution to the limits to which the bourgeoisie is prepared to go. Such people defeat their abstract Marxian revolutionary phrases by their concrete anti-Marxian and anti-revolutionary resolutions.

Those who really understand the role of the peasantry in a victorious Russian revolution would not dream of saying that the sweep of the revolution would be diminished if the bourgeoisie recoiled from it. For, as a matter of fact, the Russian revolution will begin to assume its real sweep, will really assume the widest revolutionary sweep possible in the epoch of bourgeois-democratic revolution, only when the bourgeoisie recoils from it and when the masses of the peasantry come out as active revolutionaries side by side with the proletariat. In order that it may be consistently carried to its conclusion, our democratic revolution must rely on such forces as are capable of paralyzing the inevitable inconsistency of the bourgeoisie (i.e., capable precisely of "causing it to recoil from the revolution," which the Caucasian adherents of *Iskra* fear so much because of their lack of judgment).

*The proletariat must carry to completion the democratic revolution, by allying to itself the mass of the peasantry in order to crush by force the resistance of the autocracy and to paralyze the instability of the bourgeoisie. The proletariat must accomplish the socialist revolution, by allying to itself the mass of the semiproletarian elements of the population in order to crush by force the resistance of the bourgeoisie and to paralyze the instability of the peasantry and the petty bourgeoisie.* Such are the tasks of the proletariat, which the new *Iskra*-ists present so narrowly in all their arguments and resolutions about the sweep of the revolution.

One circumstance, however, must not be forgotten, although it is frequently lost sight of in discussions about the "sweep" of the revolution. It must not be forgotten that the point at issue is not the difficulties this problem presents, but the road along which we must seek and attain its solution. The point is not whether it is easy or difficult to make the sweep of the revolution mighty and invincible, but how we must act in order to make this sweep more powerful. It is precisely on the fundamental nature of our activity, on the direction it should take, that our views differ. We emphasize this because careless and unscrupulous people too frequently confuse two different questions, namely, the question of the direction in which the road leads, i.e., the selection of one of two different roads, and the question of how easily the goal can be reached, or of how near the goal is on the given road.

We have not dealt with this last question at all in the foregoing because it has not evoked any disagreement or divergency in the Party. But it goes without saying that the question itself is extremely important and deserves the most serious attention of all Social-Democrats. It would be a piece of unpardonable optimism to forget the difficulties which accompany the task of drawing into the movement the masses not only of the working class, but also of the peasantry.

These difficulties have more than once been the rock against which the efforts to carry a democratic revolution to completion have been wrecked; and it was the inconsistent and self-seeking bourgeoisie which triumphed most of all, because it "made capital" in the shape of monarchist protection against the people, and at the same time "preserved the virginity" of liberalism . . . or of the *Osvobozhdeniye* trend. But difficult does not mean impossible. The important thing is to be convinced that the path chosen is the correct one, and this conviction will multiply a hundredfold the revolutionary energy and revolutionary enthusiasm which can perform miracles.

How deep is the disagreement among present-day Social-Democrats on the question of the path to be chosen can be seen at once by comparing the Caucasian resolution of the new *Iskra*-ists with the resolution of the Third Congress of the Russian Social-Democratic Labour Party. The Congress resolution says: the bourgeoisie is inconsistent, it will certainly try to deprive us of the gains of the revolution. Therefore, make more energetic preparations for the fight, comrades and fellow workers! Arm yourselves, win the peasantry to your side! We shall not surrender our revolutionary gains to the self-seeking bourgeoisie without a fight. The resolution of the Caucasian new *Iskra*-ists says: the bourgeoisie is inconsistent, it may recoil from the revolution. Therefore, comrades and fellow workers, please do not think of joining a provisional government, for, if you do, the bourgeoisie will certainly recoil, and the sweep of the revolution will thereby be diminished!

One side says: push the revolution forward, to its consummation, in spite of the resistance or the passivity of the inconsistent bourgeoisie.

The other side says: do not think of carrying the revolution to completion independently, for if you do, the inconsistent bourgeoisie will recoil from it.

Are these not two diametrically opposite paths? Is it not obvious that one set of tactics absolutely excludes the other? That the first tactics are the only correct tactics of revolutionary Social-Democracy, while the second are in fact purely *Osvobozhdeniye* tactics?

## 13. CONCLUSION. DARE WE WIN?

People who are superficially acquainted with the state of affairs in Russian Social-Democracy, or who judge as mere onlookers without knowing the whole history of our internal Party struggle since the days of Economism, very often also dismiss the disagreements on tactics which have now become crystallized, especially after the Third Congress, with the simple argument that there are two natural, inevitable and quite reconcilable trends in every Social-Democratic movement. One side, they say, lays special emphasis on the ordinary, current, everyday work, on the necessity of developing propaganda and agitation, of preparing forces, deepening the movement, etc., while the other side lays emphasis on the militant, general political, revolutionary tasks of the movement, points to the necessity of armed insurrection, advances the slogans: for a revolutionary-democratic dictatorship, for a provisional revolutionary government. Neither one side nor the other should exaggerate, they say; extremes are bad, both here and there (and, generally speaking, everywhere in the world), etc., etc.

The cheap truisms of worldly (and "political" in quotation marks) wisdom, which such arguments undoubtedly contain, too often cover up a failure to understand the urgent and acute needs of the Party. Take the differences on tactics that now exist among the Russian Social-Democrats. Of course, the special emphasis laid on the everyday, routine aspect of the work, such as we observe in the new *Iskra*-ist arguments about tactics, could not in itself present any danger and could not give rise to any divergence of opinion regarding tactical slogans. But the moment you compare the resolutions of the Third Congress of the Russian Social-Democratic Labour Party with the resolutions of the Conference this divergence becomes strikingly obvious.

What, then, is the trouble? The trouble is that, in the first place, it is not enough to point abstractly to the two currents in the movement and to the harmfulness of extremes. One must know concretely what the given movement is suffering from at the given time, what constitutes the real political danger to the Party at the present time. Secondly, one must know what real political forces are profiting by this or that tactical slogan — or perhaps by the absence of this or that slogan. To listen to the new *Iskra*-ists, one would arrive at the conclusion that the Social-Democratic Party is threatened with the danger of throwing overboard propaganda and agitation, the economic struggle and criticism of bourgeois democracy, of becoming inordinately absorbed in military preparations, armed attacks, the seizure of power, etc. Actually, however, real danger is threatening the Party from an entirely different quarter. Anyone who is at all closely familiar with the state of the movement, anyone who follows it carefully and thoughtfully, cannot fail to see the ridiculous side of the new *Iskra*'s fears. The entire work of the Russian Social-Democratic Labour Party has already been fully moulded into firm, immutable forms which absolutely guarantee that our main attention will be fixed on propaganda and agitation, impromptu and mass meetings, on the distribution of leaflets and pamphlets, assisting in the economic struggle and championing the slogans of that struggle. There is not a single Party committee, not a single district committee, not a single central delegates' meeting or a single factory group where ninety-nine per cent of all the attention, energy and time are not always and constantly devoted to these functions, which have become firmly established ever since the middle of the 'nineties. Only those who are entirely unfamiliar with the movement are ignorant of this. Only very naive or ill-informed people can be taken in by the new *Iskra*-ists' repetition of stale truths when it is done with an air of great importance.

The fact is that not only is no excessive zeal displayed among us with regard to the tasks of insurrection, to the general political slogans and to the matter of leading the entire popular revolution, but, on the contrary, it is *backwardness* in this very respect that stands out most strikingly, constitutes our weakest spot and a real danger to the movement, which may degenerate, and in some places is degenerating, from one that is revolutionary in deeds into one that is revolutionary in words. Among the many, many hundreds of organizations, groups and circles that are conducting the work of the Party you will not find a single one which has not from its very inception conducted the kind of everyday work about which the wiseacres of the new *Iskra* now talk with the air of people who have discovered new truths. On the other hand, you will find only an insignificant percentage of groups and circles that have understood the tasks an armed insurrection entails, which have begun to carry them out, and have realized the necessity of leading the entire popular revolution against tsarism, the necessity of advancing for that purpose certain definite progressive slogans and no other.

We are incredibly behind in our progressive and genuinely revolutionary tasks, in very many instances we have not even become conscious of them; here and there we have failed to notice the strengthening of revolutionary bourgeois democracy owing to our backwardness in this respect. But the writers in the new *Iskra,* turning their backs on the course of events and on the requirements of the times, keep repeating insistently: Don't forget the old! Don't let yourselves be carried away by the new! This is the principal and unvarying leitmotif of all the important resolutions of the Conference; whereas in the Congress resolutions you just as unvaryingly read: while confirming the old (and without stopping to chew it over and over, for the very reason that it is old and has already been settled and recorded in literature, in resolutions and by experience), we put forward a new task, draw attention to it, issue a new slogan, and demand that the genuinely revolutionary Social-Democrats immediately set to work to put it into effect.

That is how matters really stand with regard to the question of the two trends in Social-Democratic tactics. The revolutionary period has called forth new tasks, which only the totally blind can fail to see. And some Social-Democrats unhesitatingly recognize these tasks and place them on the order of the day, declaring: the armed insurrection brooks no delay, prepare yourselves for it immediately and energetically, remember that it is indispensable for a decisive victory, issue the slogans of a republic, of a provisional government, of a revolutionary-democratic dictatorship of the proletariat and the peasantry. Others, however, draw back, mark time, write prefaces instead of giving slogans; instead of pointing to the new while confirming the old, they chew this old tediously and at great length, inventing pretexts to avoid the new, unable to determine the conditions for a decisive victory or to issue the slogans which alone are in line with the striving to attain complete victory.

The political result of this *khvostism* stares us in the face. The fable about a rapprochement between the "majority" of the Russian Social-Democratic Labour Party and the revolutionary bourgeois democracy remains a fable which has not been confirmed by a single political fact, by a single important resolution of the "Bolsheviks" or a single act of the Third Congress of the Russian Social-Democratic Labour Party. On the other hand, the opportunist, monarchist bourgeoisie, as represented by the *Osvobozhdeniye*, has long been *welcoming* the trends of the "principles" of new *Iskra*-ism and now it is actually running its mill with their grist, is adopting their catchwords and "ideas" directed against "secrecy" and "riots," against exaggerating the "technical" side of the revolution, against openly proclaiming the slogan of armed insurrection, against the "revolutionism" of extreme demands, etc., etc. The resolution of a whole conference of "Menshevik" Social-Democrats in the Caucasus, and the endorsement of that resolution by the editors of the new *Iskra*, sums it all up politically in an unmistakable way: lest the bourgeoisie recoil if the proletariat takes part in a revolutionary-democratic dictatorship! This puts it in a nutshell. This gives the finishing touch to the transformation of the proletariat into an appendage of the monarchist bourgeoisie. The *political meaning* of the *khvost-*

*ism* of the new *Iskra* is thereby proved in fact, not by a casual declaration of some individual, but by a resolution especially endorsed by a whole trend.

Anyone who ponders over these facts will understand the real significance of the stock reference to the two sides and the two trends in the Social-Democratic movement. For a study of these trends on a large scale, take Bernsteinism. The Bernsteinians have been dinning into our ears in exactly the same way that it is they who understand the true needs of the proletariat, the tasks connected with the growth of its forces, with rendering the entire activity more profound, with preparing the elements of a new society, with propaganda and agitation! Bernstein says: we demand a frank recognition of what is, thus sanctifying a "movement" *without* "final aims," sanctifying defensive tactics only, preaching the tactics of fear "lest the bourgeoisie recoil." The Bernsteinians also raised an outcry against the "Jacobinism" of the revolutionary Social-Democrats, against the "publicists" who fail to understand the "initiative of the workers," etc., etc. In reality, as everyone knows, the revolutionary Social-Democrats have never even thought of abandoning the everyday, petty work, the mustering of forces, etc., etc. All they demanded was a clear understanding of the final aim, a clear presentation of the revolutionary tasks; they wanted to raise the semiproletarian and semi-petty-bourgeois strata to the revolutionary level of the proletariat, not to reduce this level to that of opportunist considerations such as "lest the bourgeoisie recoil." Perhaps the most vivid expression of this rift between the intellectual opportunist wing and the proletarian revolutionary wing of the Party was the question: dürfen wir siegen? "Dare we win?" Is it permissible for us to win? Would it not be dangerous for us to win? Ought we to win? This question, which seems so strange at first sight, was raised, however, and had to be raised, because the opportunists were afraid of victory, were frightening the proletariat away from it, were predicting that trouble would come of it, were ridiculing the slogans that straightforwardly called for it.

The same fundamental division into an intellectual opportunist and proletarian-revolutionary trend exists also among us, with the very material difference, however, that here we are faced with the question of a democratic revolution, and not of a socialist revolution. The question "dare we win?" which seems so absurd at first sight, has been raised among us also. It was raised by Martynov in his *Two Dictatorships,* in which he prophesied dire misfortune if we prepare well for and carry out an insurrection quite successfully. The question has been raised in all the new *Iskra* literature dealing with a provisional revolutionary government, and all the time persistent though futile efforts have been made to liken Millerand's participation in a bourgeois-opportunist government to Varlin's[42] participation in a petty-bourgeois revolutionary government. It is embodied in a resolution: "lest the bourgeoisie recoil." And although Kautsky, for instance, now tries to wax ironical and says that our dispute about a provisional revolutionary government is like dividing the skin of a bear before the bear has been killed, this irony only proves that even clever and revolutionary Social-Democrats are liable to put their foot in it when they talk about something they know of only by hearsay. German Social-Democracy is not yet so near to killing its bear (carrying out a socialist revolution), but the dispute as to whether we "dare" kill the bear was of enormous importance from the point of view of principles and of practical politics. Russian Social-Democrats are not yet so near to being strong enough to "kill their bear" (to carry out a democratic revolution), but the question as to whether we "dare" kill it is of extreme importance for the whole future of Russia and for the future of Russian Social-Democracy. An army cannot be energetically and successfully mustered and led unless we are sure that we "dare" win.

Take our old Economists. They too howled that their opponents were conspirators, Jacobins (see the *Rabocheye Dyelo,* especially No. 10, and Martynov's speech in the debate on the program at the Second Congress), that by plunging into politics they were divorcing themselves from the masses, that they were losing sight of the fundamentals of the working-class movement, ignoring the initiative of the workers, etc., etc. In reality these supporters of the "initiative of the workers" were opportunist intellectuals who tried to foist on the workers their own narrow and philistine conception of the tasks of the proletariat. In reality the opponents of Economism, as everyone can see from the old *Iskra,* did not neglect or push into the background any of the aspects of Social-Democratic work, nor did they in the least forget the economic struggle; but they were able at the same time to present the urgent and immediate political tasks in their full scope and they opposed the transformation of the workers' party into an "economic" appendage of the liberal bourgeoisie.

The Economists had learned by rote that politics are based on economics and "understood" this to mean that the political struggle should be reduced to the level of the economic struggle. The new *Iskra*-ists have learned by rote that the economic basis of the democratic revolution is the bourgeois revolution, and "understood" this to mean that the democratic aims of the proletariat should be degraded to the level of bourgeois moderation, to the limits beyond which "the bourgeoisie will recoil." On the pretext of rendering their work more profound, on the pretext of rousing the initiative of the workers and pursuing a purely class policy, the Economists were actually delivering the working class into the hands of the liberal-bourgeois politicians, i.e., were leading the Party along a path which objectively meant exactly that. On the same pretexts, the new *Iskra*-ists are actually betraying the interests of the proletariat in the democratic revolution to the bourgeoisie, i.e., are leading the Party along a path which objectively means exactly that. The Economists thought that leadership in the political struggle was no concern of the Social-Democrats but properly the business of the liberals. The new *Iskra*-ists think that the active conduct of the democratic revolution is no concern of the Social-Democrats but properly the business of the democratic bourgeoisie, for, they argue, if the proletariat takes the leading and pre-eminent part it will "diminish the sweep" of the revolution.

In short, the new *Iskra*-ists are the epigones of Economism, not only in their origin at the Second Party Congress, but also in the manner in which they now present the tactical tasks of the proletariat in the democratic revolution. They, too, constitute an intellectual-opportunist wing of the Party. In the sphere of organization they made their debut with the anarchist individualism of intellectuals and finished with "disorganization-as-a-process," fixing in the "Rules" adopted by the Conference[43] the separation of the Party's publishing activities from the Party organization, an indirect and practically four-stage system of elections, a system of Bonapartist plebiscites instead of democratic representation, and finally the principle of "agreements" between the part and the whole. In Party tactics they continued to slide down the same inclined plane. In the "plan of the Zemstvo campaign" they declared that speeches to Zemstvo-ists were "the highest type of demonstration," finding only two active forces on the political scene (on the eve of January 9!) — the government and the democratic bourgeoisie. They made the pressing problem of arming "more profound" by substituting for the direct and practical slogan of an appeal to arm, the slogan: arm the people with a burning desire to arm themselves. The tasks connected with an armed insurrection, with the establishment of a provisional government and with a revolutionary-democratic dictatorship have now been distorted and blunted by them in their official resolutions. "Lest the bourgeoisie recoil" — this final chord of their last resolution throws a glaring light on the question of where their path is leading the Party.

The democratic revolution in Russia is a bourgeois revolution by reason of its social and economic content. But a mere repetition of this correct Marxian proposition is not enough. It must be properly understood and properly applied in political slogans. In general, all political liberties that are founded on present-day, i.e., capitalist, relations of production are bourgeois liberties. The demand for liberty expresses primarily the interests of the bourgeoisie. Its representatives were the first to raise this demand. Its supporters have everywhere used the liberty they acquired like masters, reducing it to moderate and meticulous bourgeois doses, combining it with the most subtle methods of suppressing the revolutionary proletariat in peaceful times and with brutally cruel methods in stormy times.

But only the rebel Narodniks, the anarchists and the "Economists" could deduce from this that the struggle for liberty should be rejected or disparaged. These intellectual-philistine doctrines could be foisted on the proletariat only for a time and against its will. The proletariat always realized instinctively that it needed political liberty, needed it more than anyone else, despite the fact that its immediate effect would be to strengthen and to organize the bourgeoisie. The proletariat expects to find its salvation not by avoiding the class struggle but by developing it, by widening it, increasing its consciousness, its organization and determination. Whoever degrades the tasks of the political struggle transforms the Social-Democrat from a tribune of the people into a trade union secretary. Whoever degrades the proletarian tasks in a democratic bourgeois revolution transforms the Social-Democrat from a leader of the people's revolution into a leader of a free labour union.

Yes, the *people's* revolution. Social-Democracy has fought, and is quite rightly fighting against the bourgeois-democratic abuse of the word "people." It demands that this word shall not be used to cover up failure to understand the class antagonisms within the people. It insists categorically on the need for complete class independence for the party of the proletariat. But it divides the "people" into "classes," not in order that the advanced class may become shut up within itself, confine itself to narrow aims and emasculate its activity for fear that the economic rulers of the world will recoil, but in order that the advanced class, which does not suffer from the halfheartedness, vacillation and indecision of the intermediate classes, may with all the greater energy and enthusiasm fight for the cause of the whole of the people, at the head of the whole of the people.

That is what the present-day new *Iskra*-ists so often fail to understand and why they substitute for active political slogans in the democratic revolution a mere pedantic repetition of the word "class," parsed in all genders and cases!

The democratic revolution is a bourgeois revolution. The slogan of a Black Redistribution, or "land and liberty" — this most widespread slogan of the peasant masses, down-trodden and ignorant, yet passionately yearning for light and happiness — is a bourgeois slogan. But we Marxists should know that there is not, nor can there be, any other path to real freedom for the proletariat and the peasantry, than the path of bourgeois freedom and bourgeois progress. We must not forget that there is not, nor can there be, at the present time, any other means of bringing Socialism nearer, than complete political liberty, than a democratic republic, than the revolutionary-democratic dictatorship of the pro-letariat and the peasantry. As the representatives of the advanced and only revolutionary class, revolutionary without reservations, doubts or looking back, we must present to the whole of the people, as widely, as boldly and with the utmost initiative possible, the tasks of the democratic revolution. To degrade these tasks in theory means making a travesty of Marxism, distorting it in philistine fashion, while in practical politics it means delivering the cause of the revolution into the hands of the bourgeoisie, which will inevitably recoil from the task of consistently carrying out the revolution. The difficulties that lie on the road to the complete victory of the revolution are very great. No one will be able to blame the representatives of the proletariat if, having done everything in their power, their efforts are defeated by the resistance of the reaction, the treachery of the bourgeoisie and the ignorance of the masses. But everybody, and the class-conscious proletariat above all, will condemn Social-Democracy if it curtails the revolutionary energy of the democratic revolution and dampens revolutionary ardour because it is afraid to win, because it is actuated by the consideration: lest the bourgeoisie recoil.

Revolutions are the locomotives of history, said Marx.[44] Revolutions are the festivals of the oppressed and the exploited. At no other time are the masses of the people in a position to come forward so actively as creators of a new social order as at a time of revolution. At such times the people are capable of performing miracles, if judged by the narrow, philistine scale of gradual progress. But the leaders of the revolutionary parties must also make their aims more comprehensive and bold at such a time, so that their slogans shall always be in advance of the revolutionary initiative of the masses, serve as a beacon, reveal to them our democratic and socialist ideal in all its magnitude and splendour and show them the shortest and most direct route to complete, absolute and decisive victory. Let us leave to the opportunists of the *Osvobozhdeniye* bourgeoisie the task of inventing roundabout, circuitous paths of compromise out of fear of the revolution and of the direct path. If we are compelled by force to drag ourselves along such paths, we shall be able to fulfil our duty in petty, everyday work also. But let ruthless struggle first decide the choice of the path. We shall be traitors to and betrayers of the revolution if we do not use this festive energy of the masses and their revolutionary ardour to wage a ruthless and self-sacrificing struggle for the direct and decisive path. Let the bourgeois opportunists contemplate the future reaction with craven fear. The workers will not be frightened either by the thought that the reaction promises to be terrible or by the thought that the bourgeoisie proposes to recoil. The workers are not looking forward to striking bargains, are not asking for sops; they are striving to crush the reactionary forces without mercy, i.e., to set up the *revolutionary-democratic dictatorship of the proletariat and the peasantry.*

Of course, greater dangers threaten the ship of our Party in stormy times than in periods of the smooth "sailing" of liberal progress, which means the painfully slow sweating of the working class by its exploiters. Of course, the tasks of the revolutionary-democratic dictatorship are a thousand times more difficult and more complicated than the tasks of an "extreme opposition" or of the exclusively parliamentary struggle. But whoever can deliberately prefer smooth sailing and the path of safe "opposition" in the present revolutionary situation had better abandon Social-Democratic work for a while, had better wait until the revolution is over, until the festive days have passed, when humdrum everyday life starts again and his narrow routine standards no longer strike such an abominably discordant note, or constitute such an ugly distortion of the tasks of the advanced class.

At the head of the whole of the people, and particularly of the peasantry — for complete freedom, for a consistent democratic revolution, for a republic! At the head of all the toilers and the exploited — for Socialism! Such must in practice be the policy of the revolutionary proletariat, such is the class slogan which must permeate and determine the solution of every tactical problem, every practical step of the workers' party during the revolution.

## ONCE AGAIN *OSVOBOZHDENIYE*-ISM, ONCE AGAIN NEW *ISKRA*-ISM

Numbers 71-72 of the *Osvobozhdeniye* and Nos. 102-103 of the *Iskra* provide a wealth of additional material on the question to which we have devoted Chapter 8 of our pamphlet. Since it is quite impossible to make use of the whole of this rich material here, we shall confine ourselves to the most important points only: firstly, to the kind of "realism" in Social-Democracy that *Osvobozhdeniye* praises and why the latter must praise it; secondly, to the relationship between the concepts revolution and dictatorship.

## I. WHAT DO THE BOURGEOIS LIBERAL REALISTS PRAISE THE SOCIAL-DEMOCRATIC "REALISTS" FOR?

The articles entitled "The Split in Russian Social-Democracy" and "The Triumph of Common Sense" (*Osvobozhdeniye*, No. 72) set forth the opinion on Social-Democracy held by the representatives of the liberal bourgeoisie, an opinion which is of remarkable value for class-conscious proletarians. We cannot too strongly recommend every Social-Democrat to read these articles in full and to *ponder over* every sentence in them. We shall reproduce first of all the most important propositions contained in both these articles.

"It is fairly difficult," writes the *Osvobozhdeniye*, "for an outside observer to grasp the real political meaning of the disagreements that have split the Social-Democratic Party into two factions. A definition of the 'Majority' faction as the more radical and unswerving, as distinct from the 'Minority' which allows of certain compromises in the interests of the cause, would not be quite exact, and in any case would not provide an exhaustive characterization. At any rate the traditional dogmas of Marxian orthodoxy are observed by the Minority faction with even greater zeal perhaps than by the Lenin faction. The following characterization would appear to us to be more accurate. The fundamental political temper of the 'Majority' is abstract revolutionism, rebellion for the sake of rebellion, an eagerness to stir up insurrection among the popular masses by any and every means and to seize power immediately in their name; to a certain extent this brings the 'Leninists' close to the Socialist-Revolutionaries and overshadows in their minds the idea of the class struggle with the idea of a Russian revolution involving the whole people; while abjuring in practice much of the narrow-mindedness of the Social-Democratic doctrine, the 'Leninists' are, on the other hand, thoroughly imbued with the narrow-mindedness of revolutionism, renounce all practical work except the preparation of an immediate insurrection, ignore on principle all forms of legal and semilegal agitation and every species of practically-useful compromise with other oppositional trends. The Minority, on the contrary, while steadfastly adhering to the doctrine of Marxism, at the same time preserves the realistic elements of the Marxian world outlook. The fundamental idea of this faction is to oppose the interests of the 'proletariat' to the interests of the bourgeoisie. But, on the other hand, the struggle of the proletariat is conceived — of course within certain bounds dictated by the immutable dogmas of Social-Democracy — in realistically sober fashion, with a clear realization of all the concrete conditions and aims of this struggle. Neither of the two factions pursues its basic point of view quite consistently, for in their ideological and political activity they are bound by the strict formulae of the Social-Democratic catechism, which keep the 'Leninists' from becoming unswerving rebels, after the fashion of some, at least, of the Socialist-Revolutionaries, and the '*Iskra*-ists' from becoming the practical leaders of the real political movement of the working class."

And, after quoting the contents of the most important resolutions, the *Osvobozhdeniye* writer goes on to illustrate his general "thoughts," with several concrete remarks about them. In comparison with the Third Congress, he says, "the Minority Conference takes a totally different attitude towards armed insurrection." "In connection with the attitude towards armed insurrection," there is a difference in the respective resolutions on a provisional government. "A similar difference is revealed in relation to the workers' trade unions. The 'Leninists' do not say a single word in their resolution about this most important starting point in the political education and organization of the working class. The Minority, on the other hand, drew up a very weighty resolution." With regard to the liberals, both factions, he says, are unanimous, but the Third Congress "repeats almost word for word Plekhanov's resolution on the attitude towards the liberals adopted at the Second Congress and rejects Starover's resolution adopted by the same Congress, which was more favourably inclined towards the liberals." Although the Congress and the Conference resolutions on the peasant movement coincide on the whole, "the 'Majority' lays more emphasis on the idea of the revolutionary confiscation of the landlords' estates and other land, while the 'Minority' wants to make the demand for democratic state and administrative reforms the basis of its agitation."

Finally, the *Osvobozhdeniye* cites from the *Iskra*, No. 100, a Menshevik resolution, the main clause of which reads as follows: "In view of the fact that at the present time underground work alone does not secure adequate participation of the masses in Party life and in some degree leads to the masses as such being contrasted to the Party as an illegal organization, the latter must assume leadership of the trade union struggle of the workers on a legal basis, strictly linking up this struggle with the Social-Democratic tasks." Commenting on this resolution the *Osvobozhdeniye* exclaims: "We heartily welcome this resolution as a triumph of common sense, as evidence that a definite section of the Social-Democratic Party is beginning to see the light with regard to tactics."

The reader now has before him all the essential opinions of the *Osvobozhdeniye*. It would, of course, be the greatest mistake to regard these opinions as correct in the sense that they correspond to objective truth. Every Social-

Democrat will easily detect mistakes in them at every step. It would be naive to forget that these opinions are thoroughly permeated with the interests and the points of view of the liberal bourgeoisie, and that accordingly they are utterly biassed and tendentious. They reflect the views of the Social-Democrats in the same way as objects are reflected in a concave or convex mirror. But it would be an even greater mistake to forget that in the final analysis these bourgeois-distorted opinions reflect the real interests of the bourgeoisie, which, as a class, undoubtedly understands correctly which trends in Social-Democracy are advantageous, close, akin and agreeable, and which trends are harmful, distant, alien and antipathetic to it. A bourgeois philosopher or a bourgeois publicist can never understand Social-Democracy properly, neither Menshevik nor Bolshevik Social-Democracy. But if he is at all a sensible publicist, his class instinct will not deceive him, and he will always grasp the significance for the bourgeoisie of one or another trend in the Social-Democratic movement, on the whole correctly, although he may present it in a distorted way. That is why the class instinct of our enemy, his class opinion, is always deserving of the most serious attention of every class-conscious proletarian.

What, then, does the class instinct of the Russian bourgeoisie, as expressed by the *Osvobozhdentsi*, tell us?

It quite definitely expresses its satisfaction with the trend represented by the new *Iskra,* praises it for its realism, sober-mindedness, the triumph of common sense, the seriousness of its resolutions, its beginning to see the light on questions of tactics, its practicalness, etc. — and it expresses dissatisfaction with the trend of the Third Congress, censures it for its narrow-mindedness, revolutionism, its rebel spirit, its repudiation of practically useful compromises, etc. The class instinct of the bourgeoisie suggests to it exactly what has been repeatedly proved with the help of most precise facts in our literature, namely, that the new *Iskra*-ists are the opportunist and their opponents the revolutionary wing of the present-day Russian Social-Democratic movement. The liberals cannot but sympathize with the trend of the former, and cannot but censure the trend of the latter. The liberals, being the ideologists of the bourgeoisie, perfectly well understand the advantages to the bourgeoisie of "practicalness, sober-mindedness and seriousness" on the part of the working class, i.e., of actually restricting its field of activity within the boundaries of capitalism, reforms, the trade union struggle, etc. Dangerous and terrible to the bourgeoisie is the "revolutionary narrow-mindedness" of the proletariat and its endeavour in order to promote its own class aims to win the leadership in a popular Russian revolution.

That this is the real meaning of the word "realism" as employed by the *Osvobozhdeniye* is evident among other things from the way it was used previously by the *Osvobozhdeniye* and Mr. Struve. The *Iskra* itself could not but admit that *this* was the meaning of the *Osvobozhdeniye*'s "realism." Take, for instance, the article entitled "It Is High Time!" in the supplement to the *Iskra,* No. 73-74. The author of this article (a consistent exponent of the views of the "Marsh" at the Second Congress of the Russian Social-Democratic Labour Party) frankly expressed the opinion that "at the Congress Akimov played the part of the ghost of opportunism rather than of its real representative." And the editors of the *Iskra* were forthwith obliged to correct the author of the article "It Is High Time!" by stating in a note:

"We cannot agree with this opinion. Comrade Akimov's views on the program bear the clear imprint of opportunism, which fact is admitted even by the *Osvobozhdeniye* critic, who — in one of its recent issues — stated that Comrade Akimov is an adherent of the 'realist' — read: revisionist — tendency."

Thus the *Iskra* itself is perfectly aware that the *Osvobozhdeniye*'s "realism" is simply opportunism and nothing else. If in attacking "liberal realism" (*Iskra*, No. 102) the *Iskra* now says nothing about how *it was praised by the liberals* for its realism, the explanation of this circumstance is that such praise is harder to swallow than any censure. Such praise (which the *Osvobozhdeniye* uttered not by mere chance and not for the first time) actually proves the affinity between liberal realism and those tendencies of Social-Democratic "realism" (read: opportunism) that run through every resolution of the new *Iskra*-ists as a result of the mistaken character of their whole tactical line.

Indeed, the Russian bourgeoisie has already fully revealed its inconsistency and egoism in the "popular" revolution — has revealed it in Mr. Struve's arguments, by the whole tone and content of the numerous liberal newspapers, and by the nature of the political utterances of the bulk of the Zemstvo-ists, the bulk of the intellectuals and in general of all the adherents of Messrs. Trubetskoy, Petrunkevich, Rodichev and Co. Of course, the bourgeoisie does not always clearly understand, but in general and on the whole, its class instinct enables it to grasp perfectly well that, on the one hand, the proletariat and the "people" are useful for *its* revolution as cannon fodder, as a battering-ram against the autocracy, but that, on the other hand, the proletariat and the revolutionary peasantry will be terribly dangerous to it if they win a "decisive victory over tsarism" and carry the democratic revolution to completion. That is why the bourgeoisie strains every effort to induce the proletariat to be content with a "modest" role in the revolution, to be more sober-minded, practical and realistic, to be guided in its activities by the principle, "lest the bourgeoisie recoil."

The bourgeois intellectuals know full well that they will not be able to get rid of the working-class movement. That is why they do not come out against the working-class movement, they do not come out against the class struggle of the proletariat — no, they even pay lip service to the right to strike, to a genteel class struggle, understanding the working-class movement and the class struggle in the Brentano or Hirsch-Duncker sense. In other words they are fully prepared to "yield" to the workers the right to strike and to organize in trade unions (which in fact has already been almost won by the workers themselves), provided the workers renounce their "rebelliousness," their "narrow-minded revolutionism," their hostility to "practically-useful compromises," their claims and aspirations to put on the "popular Russian revolution," the imprint of *their* class struggle, the imprint of proletarian consistency, proletarian determination and "plebeian Jacobinism." That is why the bourgeois intellectuals all over Russia exert every effort, resort to thousands of ways and means — books,* lectures, speeches, talks, etc., etc. — to imbue the workers with the ideas of (bourgeois) sober-mindedness, (liberal) practicalness, (opportunist) realism, (Brentano) class struggle, (Hirsch-Duncker) trade unions,[45] etc. The latter two slogans are

---

* Cf. Prokopovich, *The Labour Question in Russia.*

particularly convenient for the bourgeois of the "constitutional-democratic" party, or the party of "liberation," since outwardly they coincide with the Marxian slogans, since with a few small omissions and some slight distortions they can easily be confused with and sometimes even passed off as Social-Democratic slogans. For instance, the legal liberal newspaper *Rassvyet* (which we will try some day to discuss in greater detail with the readers of the *Proletary*) frequently says such "bold" things about the class struggle, about the possible deception of the proletariat by the bourgeoisie, about the working-class movement, about the initiative of the proletariat, etc., etc., that the inattentive reader or an unenlightened worker might easily be led to believe that its "social-democratism" is genuine. Actually, however, it is a bourgeois imitation of social-democratism, an opportunist distortion and perversion of the concept class struggle.

At the bottom of the whole of this gigantic (in breadth of influence on the masses) bourgeois subterfuge lies the tendency to reduce the working-class movement mainly to a trade union movement, to keep it as far away as possible from an independent (i.e., revolutionary and directed towards a democratic dictatorship) policy, to "overshadow in the minds of the workers the idea of a Russian revolution involving the whole people with the idea of the class struggle."

As the reader will perceive, we have turned the *Osvobozhdeniye* formulation upside down. This is an excellent formulation that excellently expresses the two views of the role of the proletariat in a democratic revolution: the bourgeois view and the Social-Democratic view. The bourgeoisie wants to confine the proletariat to the trade union movement and thereby to "overshadow in its mind the idea of a Russian revolution involving the whole people with the idea of the (*Brentano*) class struggle" — which is wholly in the spirit of the Bernsteinian authors of the *Credo*, who overshadowed in the minds of the workers the idea of political struggle with the idea of a "purely working-class" movement.  Social-Democracy, however, wants, on the contrary, to develop the class struggle of the proletariat to the point where the latter will take the leading part in the popular Russian revolution, i.e., will lead this revolution to the democratic dictatorship of the proletariat and the peasantry.

The revolution in our country is one that involves the whole people, says the bourgeoisie to the proletariat. Therefore, you, as a separate class, must confine yourselves to your class struggle, must in the name of "common sense" devote your attention mainly to the trade unions, and their legalization, must consider these trade unions as "the most important starting point in your political education and organization," must in a revolutionary situation draw up for the most part "serious" resolutions like the new *Iskra* resolution, must pay careful heed to resolutions that are "more favourably inclined towards the liberals," must show preference for leaders who display a tendency to become "practical leaders of the real political movement of the working class," must "preserve the realistic elements of the Marxian world outlook" (if you have unfortunately already become infected with the "strict formulae" of this "unscientific" catechism).

The revolution in our country is one involving the whole people, Social-Democracy says to the proletariat.  Therefore, you, as the most progressive and the only thoroughly revolutionary class, must strive not only to take the most active part, but also the leading part in it.  Therefore, you must not confine yourselves to narrowly conceived limits of the class struggle, meaning mainly the trade union movement, but, on the contrary, you must strive to widen the limits and the content of your class struggle to *include* not only *all* the aims of the present, democratic, Russian revolution of the whole of the people, but the aims of the subsequent socialist revolution as well. Therefore, while not ignoring the trade union movement, while not refusing to take advantage of even the slightest legal possibilities, you must, in a revolutionary period, put in the forefront the tasks of armed insurrection and the formation of a revolutionary army and a revolutionary government as being the only way to the complete victory of the people over tsarism, to the winning of a democratic republic and real political liberty.

It would be superfluous to speak about the halfhearted and inconsistent stand, which, naturally, is so pleasing to the bourgeoisie, that the new *Iskra*-ist resolutions took on this question because of their mistaken "line."

## II. COMRADE MARTYNOV AGAIN RENDERS THE QUESTION "MORE PROFOUND"

Let us pass on to Martynov's articles in Nos. 102 and 103 of the *Iskra*. We shall, of course, make no reply to Martynov's attempts to prove the incorrectness of our and the correctness of his interpretation of a number of citations from Engels and Marx. These attempts are so trivial, Martynov's subterfuges so obvious and the question so clear that it would be of no interest to dwell on this point again. Every thinking reader will be able easily to see through the simple wiles employed by Martynov in his retreat all along the line, particularly when the complete translations of Engels' pamphlet *The Bakuninists at Work* and Marx's *Address of the Central Council to the Communist League* of March 1850,[46] on which a group of collaborators of the *Proletary* are now working, are published. A single quotation from Martynov's article will suffice to make his retreat clear to the reader.

"The *Iskra* admits," says Martynov in No. 103, "that the establishment of a provisional government is one of the possible and expedient ways of furthering the revolution, and denies the expediency of the participation of Social-Democrats in a *bourgeois* provisional government, precisely in the interests of a complete seizure, in the future, of the state machine for a socialist revolution." In other words, the *Iskra* now admits the absurdity of all its fears concerning the responsibility of a revolutionary government for the exchequer and the banks, concerning the danger and impossibility of taking over the "prisons," etc. But the *Iskra* is only muddling things as of old, confusing the democratic with the socialist dictatorship. This muddle is unavoidable, it is a means to cover up the retreat.

But among the muddleheads of the new *Iskra* Martynov stands out as a muddlehead of the first order, as a muddlehead of talent, if we may so express it. Confusing the question by his laborious efforts to render it "more profound," he almost invariably "arrives at" new formulations which show up splendidly the entire falsity of the stand he has taken. You will remember how in the days of Economism he rendered Plekhanov "more profound" and created the formulation: "economic struggle against the employers and the government." It would be difficult to find in all the literature of the Economists a more apt expression of the entire falsity of this trend. It is the same today. Martynov zealously serves the new *Iskra* and almost every time he opens his mouth he furnishes us with new and excellent material for an evaluation of the new *Iskra*'s false position. In No. 102 he says that Lenin "has imperceptibly substituted the concept dictatorship for that of revolution" (p. 3, col. 2).

As a matter of fact all the accusations levelled at us by the new *Iskra*-ists can be reduced to this one. And how grateful we are to Martynov for this accusation! What an invaluable service he renders us in the struggle against the new *Iskra* ideas by formulating his accusation in this way! We must positively beg the editors of the *Iskra* to let Martynov loose against us more often for the purpose of rendering the attacks on the *Proletary* "more profound" and for a "truly principled" formulation of these attacks. For the more Martynov strains to argue on the plane of principles the worse his arguments appear, and the more clearly he reveals the gaps in the new *Iskra* ideas, the more successfully he performs on himself and on his friends the useful pedagogical operation: reductio ad absurdum (reducing the principles of the new *Iskra* to absurdity).

The *Vperyod* and the *Proletary* "substitute" the term dictatorship for that of revolution. The *Iskra* does not want such a "substitution." Just so, most esteemed Comrade Martynov! You have unwittingly stated a great truth. With this *new* formulation you have confirmed our contention that the *Iskra* is dragging at the tail of the revolution, is straying into an *Osvobozhdeniye* formulation of its tasks, whereas the *Vperyod* and the *Proletary* are issuing slogans that lead the democratic revolution forward.

You don't understand this, Comrade Martynov? In view of the importance of the question we shall try to give you a detailed explanation.

The bourgeois character of the democratic revolution expresses itself, among other things, in the fact that a number of classes, groups and sections of society which take their stand entirely on the recognition of private property and commodity production and are incapable of going beyond these bounds, are led by force of circumstances to recognize the uselessness of the autocracy and of the whole feudal order in general, and join in the demand for liberty. The bourgeois character of *this* liberty, which is demanded by "society" and advocated in a flood of words (and words only!) by the landowners and the capitalists, is manifesting itself more and more clearly. At the same time the radical difference between the struggle of the workers and the struggle of the bourgeoisie for liberty, between proletarian and liberal democratism, also becomes more obvious. The working class and its class-conscious representatives are marching forward and pushing this struggle forward, not only without fearing to carry it to completion, but striving to go far beyond the uttermost limits of the democratic revolution. The bourgeoisie is inconsistent and self-seeking, and accepts the slogans of liberty only in part and hypocritically. All attempts to draw a particular line or to draw up particular "points" (like the points in Starover's or the Conferencers' resolution) beyond which begins this hypocrisy of the bourgeois friends of liberty, or, if you like, this betrayal of liberty by its bourgeois friends, are inevitably doomed to failure; for the bourgeoisie, caught between two fires (the autocracy and the proletariat), is capable of changing its position and slogans by a thousand ways and means, of adapting itself by moving an inch to the Left or an inch to the Right, constantly bargaining and dickering. The task of proletarian democratism is not to invent such lifeless "points," but unceasingly to criticize the developing political situation, to expose the ever new and unforeseeable inconsistencies and betrayals on the part of the bourgeoisie.

Recall the history of Mr. Struve's political pronouncements in the illegal press, the history of Social-Democracy's war with him, and you will see clearly how these tasks were carried out by Social-Democracy, the champion of proletarian democratism. Mr. Struve began with a purely Shipov slogan: "Rights and an Authoritative Zemstvo" (see my article in the *Zarya*, "The Persecutors of the Zemstvo and the Hannibals of Liberalism"[47]). Social-Democracy exposed him and pushed him in the direction of a definitely constitutionalist program. When this "pushing" took effect, thanks to the particularly rapid progress of revolutionary events, the struggle shifted to the *next* question of democracy: not only a constitution in general, but one providing for universal and equal suffrage, direct elections and secret ballot. When we "captured" this new position from the "enemy" (the adoption of universal suffrage by the Osvobozhdeniye League) we began to press further; we showed up the hypocrisy and falsity of a two-chamber system, and the fact that universal suffrage had not been fully recognized by the *Osvobozhdentsi*; we pointed to their *monarchism* and showed up the huckstering nature of their democratism, or, in other words, the *bartering away* of the interests of the great Russian revolution by these *Osvobozhdeniye* heroes of the moneybags.

Finally, the savage obstinacy of the autocracy, the enormous progress of the civil war and the hopelessness of the position into which the monarchists have led Russia have begun to penetrate even the thickest skulls. The revolution has become a *fact*. It is no longer necessary to be a revolutionary to acknowledge the revolution. The autocratic government has actually been and is disintegrating in the sight of all. As has justly been remarked in the legal press by a certain liberal (Mr. Gredeskul), actual insubordination to this government has set in. Despite all its apparent strength the autocracy has proved impotent; the events attending the developing revolution have simply begun to brush aside this parasitic organism which is rotting alive. Compelled to base their activity (or, to put it more correctly, their political wire-pulling) on relationships as they are actually taking shape, the liberal bourgeois *have begun to see the necessity of recognizing the revolution*. They do so not because they are revolutionaries, but despite the fact that they are not revolutionaries. They do so of necessity and against their will, angrily glaring at the successes of the revolution, they blame the autocracy for the revolution because it does not want to strike a bargain, but wants a life-and-death struggle. Born hucksters, they hate struggle and revolution, but circumstances force them to tread the ground of revolution, for there is no other ground under their feet.

We are witnessing a highly instructive and highly comical spectacle. The bourgeois liberal prostitutes are trying to drape themselves in the toga of revolution. The *Osvobozhdentsi* — risum teneatis, amici!* — the *Osvobozhdentsi* are beginning to speak in the name of the revolution! The *Osvobozhdentsi* are beginning to assure us that they "do not fear revolution" (Mr. Struve in the *Osvobozhdeniye*, No. 72)!!! The *Osvobozhdentsi* are voicing their claims "to be at the head of the revolution"!!!

------

* Restrain your laughter, friends!

This is an exceptionally significant phenomenon that characterizes not only the progress of bourgeois liberalism, but even more so the progress of the real successes of the revolutionary movement, which has *compelled* recognition. Even the bourgeoisie is beginning to feel that it is more to its advantage to take its stand on the side of the revolution — so shaky is the autocracy. On the other hand, this phenomenon, which testifies to the fact that the entire movement has risen to a new and higher plane, also sets us new and higher tasks. The recognition of the revolution by the bourgeoisie cannot be sincere, irrespective of the personal integrity of this or that bourgeois ideologist. The bourgeoisie cannot help introducing selfishness and inconsistency, the bargaining spirit and petty reactionary tricks even into this higher stage of the movement. We must now formulate the immediate *concrete* tasks of the revolution *differently*, in the name of our program and in amplification of our program. What was adequate yesterday is *inadequate today*. Yesterday, perhaps, the demand for the recognition of the revolution was adequate as an advanced democratic slogan. Today this is not enough. The revolution has forced even Mr. Struve to recognize it. The advanced class must now define exactly *the very content* of the urgent and pressing tasks of this revolution. While recognizing the revolution, Messrs. the Struves again and again expose their asses' ears and strike up the old song about the possibility of a peaceful outcome, about *Nicholas* calling on the *Osvobozhdentsi* to take power, etc., etc. The *Osvobozhdentsi* recognize the revolution in order the more safely for themselves to conjure it away, to betray it. It is our duty at the present time to show the proletariat and the whole people the inadequacy of the slogan: "Revolution"; we must show how necessary it is to have a clear and unambiguous, consistent and determined definition of *the very content* of the revolution. And this definition is provided by the one slogan that is capable of correctly expressing a "decisive victory" of the revolution, the slogan: for the revolutionary-democratic dictatorship of the proletariat and the peasantry.

The misuse of terms[48] is a most common practice in politics. The term "Socialist," for example, has often been appropriated by the supporters of English bourgeois liberalism ("We are all Socialists now," said Harcourt), by the supporters of Bismarck, and by the friends of Pope Leo XIII. The term "revolution" also fully lends itself to misuse and at a certain stage in the development of the movement such misuse is inevitable. When Mr. Struve began to speak in the name of revolution I involuntarily remembered Thiers. A few days before the February revolution, this monstrous gnome, this most consummate expression of the political corruption of the bourgeoisie, scented the approach of a popular storm, and so he announced from the parliamentary tribune: that he was *of the party of revolution*! (See Marx's *The Civil War in France.*)[49] The political significance of *Osvobozhdeniye*'s turn to the party of revolution is *quite identical* with that of Thiers. The fact that the Russian Thiers are talking about their belonging to the party of revolution shows that the slogan revolution has become inadequate, meaningless and defines no tasks: for the revolution has become a fact, and the most diverse elements are flocking to its side.

Indeed, what is revolution from the Marxist point of view? The violent break-up of the obsolete political superstructure, the contradiction between which and the new relations of production caused its collapse at a certain moment. The contradiction between the autocracy and the entire structure of capitalist Russia, all the requirements of her bourgeois-democratic development, has now caused its collapse, all the more severe owing to the lengthy period in which this contradiction was artificially sustained. The superstructure is cracking at every joint, it is yielding to pressure, it is growing weaker. The people, through the representatives of the most diverse classes and groups, must now, by its own efforts, build a new superstructure for itself. At a certain stage of development the uselessness of the old superstructure becomes obvious to all. The revolution is recognized by all. The task now is to define *which* classes must build the new superstructure, and *how* they are to build it. If this is not defined, the slogan revolution is empty and meaningless at the present time; for the feebleness of the autocracy makes "revolutionaries" even of the Grand Dukes and of the *Moskovskiye Vyedomosti*[150] If this is not defined there can be no talk about the advanced democratic tasks of the advanced class. This definition is given in the slogan: the democratic dictatorship of the proletariat and the peasantry. This slogan defines the classes upon which the new "builders" of the new superstructure can and must rely, the character of the new superstructure (a "democratic" as distinct from a socialist dictatorship), and how it is to be built (dictatorship, i.e., the violent suppression of violent resistance, arming the revolutionary classes of the people). Whoever now refuses to recognize this slogan of revolutionary democratic dictatorship, the slogan of a revolutionary army, of a revolutionary government, of revolutionary peasant committees, either hopelessly fails to understand the tasks of the revolution, is unable to define the new and higher tasks that are called forth by the present situation, or is deceiving the people, betraying the revolution, misusing the slogan "revolution."

The former case applies to Comrade Martynov and his friends. The latter applies to Mr. Struve and the whole of the "constitutional-democratic" Zemstvo party.

Comrade Martynov was so shrewd and smart that he hurled the charge of "substituting" the term dictatorship for that of revolution just at the time when the development of the revolution called for a definition of its tasks by the slogan dictatorship! Actually, Comrade Martynov again had the misfortune to remain at the tail end, to get stranded at the penultimate stage, to *find himself on the level of Osvobozhdeniye*-ism, for it is precisely to the political stand of *Osvobozhdeniye*, i.e., to the interests of the liberal monarchist bourgeoisie, that recognition of "revolution" (in words) and refusal to recognize the democratic dictatorship of the proletariat and the peasantry (i.e., revolution in deeds) now corresponds. The liberal bourgeoisie, through the mouth of Mr. Struve, is now expressing itself in favour of revolution. The class-conscious proletariat, through the mouths of the revolutionary Social-Democrats, is demanding the dictatorship of the proletariat and the peasantry. And here the wiseacre of the new *Iskra* intervenes in the controversy and yells: don't dare "substitute" the term dictatorship for that of revolution! Well, is it not true that the false stand taken by the new *Iskra*-ists dooms them to be constantly dragging along at the tail of *Osvobozhdeniye*-ism?

We have shown that the *Osvobozhdentsi* are ascending (not without encouraging prods by the Social-Democrats) step by step in the matter of recognizing democracy. At first the issue in the dispute between us was: the Shipov system (rights and an authoritative Zemstvo) or constitutionalism? Then it was: limited suffrage or universal suffrage? Later: recognition of the revolution or a stockjobber's bargain with the autocracy? Finally, now it is: recognition of the revolution without the dictatorship of the proletariat and the peasantry or recognition of the demand for a dictatorship of these classes in the democratic revolution? It is possible and probable that Messrs. the *Osvobozhdentsi* (whether the present ones or their successors in the Left wing of the bourgeois democrats makes no difference) will ascend another step, i.e., recognize in time (perhaps by the time Comrade Martynov goes up one more step) the slogan of dictatorship also. This will inevitably be so if the Russian revolution continues to forge ahead successfully and achieves a decisive victory. What will be the position of Social-Democracy then? The complete victory of the present revolution will mark the end of the democratic revolution and the beginning of a determined struggle for a socialist revolution. The satisfaction of the demands of the present-day peasantry, the utter rout of reaction, and the winning of a democratic republic will mark the complete end of the revolutionism of the bourgeoisie and even of the petty bourgeoisie — will mark the beginning of the real struggle of the proletariat for Socialism. The more complete the democratic revolution, the sooner, the more widespread, the purer and the more determined will be the development of this new struggle. The slogan of a "democratic" dictatorship expresses the historically limited nature of the present revolution and the necessity of a new struggle on the basis of the new order for the complete emancipation of the working class from all oppression and all exploitation. In other words: when the democratic bourgeoisie or petty bourgeoisie ascends another step, when not only the revolution but the complete victory of the revolution becomes an accomplished fact, we shall "substitute" (perhaps amid the horrified cries of new, future, Martynovs) for the slogan of the democratic dictatorship, the slogan of a socialist dictatorship of the proletariat, i.e., of a complete socialist revolution.

## III. THE VULGAR BOURGEOIS REPRESENTATION OF DICTATORSHIP AND MARX'S VIEW OF IT

Mehring[51] tells us in his notes to Marx's articles from the *Neue Rheinische Zeitung* of 1848 that he published, that one of the reproaches levelled at this newspaper by bourgeois publications was that it had allegedly demanded "the immediate introduction of a dictatorship as the sole means of achieving democracy" (Marx, *Nachlass,* Vol. III, p. 53). From the vulgar bourgeois standpoint the terms dictatorship and democracy are mutually exclusive. Failing to understand the theory of class struggle, and accustomed to seeing in the political arena the petty squabbling of the various bourgeois circles and coteries, the bourgeois conceives dictatorship to mean the annulment of all the liberties and guarantees of democracy, tyranny of every kind, and every sort of abuse of power in the personal interests of a dictator. In essence, it is precisely this vulgar bourgeois view that is manifested in the writings of our Martynov, who winds up his "new campaign" in the new *Iskra* by attributing the partiality of the *Vperyod* and the *Proletary* for the slogan of dictatorship to Lenin's "passionate desire to try his luck" (*Iskra*, No. 103, p. 3, col. 2). In order to explain to Martynov the meaning of the term class dictatorship as distinct from personal dictatorship, and the tasks of a democratic dictatorship as distinct from those of a socialist dictatorship, it would not be amiss to dwell on the views of the *Neue Rheinische Zeitung*.

"Every provisional organization of the state after a revolution," wrote the *Neue Rheinische Zeitung* on September 14, 1848, "requires a dictatorship, and an energetic dictatorship at that. From the very beginning we have reproached Camphausen" (the head of the Ministry after March 18, 1848) "for not acting dictatorially, for not having immediately smashed up and eliminated the remnants of the old institutions. And while Herr Camphausen was lulling himself with constitutional illusions, the defeated party (i.e., the party of reaction) strengthened its positions in the bureaucracy, and in the army, and here and there even began to venture upon open struggle."[52]

These words, Mehring justly remarks, sum up in a few propositions all that was propounded in detail in the *Neue Rheinische Zeitung* in long articles on the Camphausen Ministry. What do these words of Marx tell us? That a provisional revolutionary government *must* act dictatorially (a proposition which the *Iskra* was totally unable to grasp since it was fighting shy of the slogan: dictatorship) and that the task of such a dictatorship is to destroy the remnants of the old institutions (which is precisely what was clearly stated in the resolution of the Third Congress of the Russian Social-Democratic Labour Party about the struggle against counterrevolution, and what was omitted in the resolution of the Conference, as we showed above). Thirdly, and lastly, it follows from these words that Marx castigated the bourgeois democrats for entertaining "constitutional illusions" in a period of revolution and open civil war. The meaning of these words becomes particularly obvious from the article in the *Neue Rheinische Zeitung* of

June 6, 1848. "A Constituent National Assembly," wrote Marx, "must first of all be an active, revolutionary-active assembly. The Frankfurt Assembly, however, is busying itself with school exercises in parliamentarism while allowing the government to act. Let us assume that this learned assembly succeeds after mature consideration in working out the best possible agenda and the best possible constitution. But what is the use of the best possible agenda and of the best possible constitution, if the German governments have in the meantime placed the bayonet on the agenda?"[53]

That is the meaning of the slogan: dictatorship. We can judge from this what Marx's attitude would have been towards resolutions which call a "decision to organize a constituent assembly" a decisive victory, or which invite us to "remain the party of extreme revolutionary opposition"!

Major questions in the life of nations are settled only by force. The reactionary classes themselves are usually the first to resort to violence, to civil war; they are the first to "place the bayonet on the agenda," as the Russian autocracy has been doing systematically and undeviatingly everywhere ever since January 9. And since such a situation has arisen, since the bayonet has really become the main point on the political agenda, since insurrection has proved to be imperative and urgent — constitutional illusions and school exercises in parliamentarism become only a screen for the bourgeois betrayal of the revolution, a screen to conceal the fact that the bourgeoisie is "recoiling" from the revolution. It is therefore the slogan of dictatorship that the genuinely revolutionary class must advance.

On the question of the tasks of this dictatorship Marx wrote, already in the *Neue Rheinische Zeitung*: "The National Assembly should have acted dictatorially against the reactionary attempts of the obsolete governments; the force of public opinion in its favour would then have been so strong as to shatter all bayonets. . . . But this Assembly bores the German people instead of carrying the people with it or being carried away by it."[54]  In Marx's opinion, the National Assembly should have "eliminated from the regime actually existing in Germany everything that contradicted the principle of the sovereignty of the people," then it should have "consolidated the revolutionary ground on which it stands in order to make the sovereignty of the people, won by the revolution, secure against all attacks."[55]

Thus, the tasks which Marx set before a revolutionary government or dictatorship in 1848 amounted in substance primarily to a *democratic* revolution: defence against counterrevolution and the actual elimination of everything that contradicted the sovereignty of the people. This is nothing else than a revolutionary-democratic dictatorship.

To proceed: which classes, in Marx's opinion, could and should have achieved this task (actually to exercise to the full the principle of the sovereignty of the people and to beat off the attacks of the counterrevolution)? Marx speaks of the "people." But we know that he always ruthlessly combated the petty-bourgeois illusions about the unity of the "people" and about the absence of a class struggle within the people. In using the word "people," Marx did not thereby gloss over class distinctions, but combined definite elements that were capable of carrying the revolution to completion.

After the victory of the Berlin proletariat on March 18, wrote the *Neue Rheinische Zeitung,* the results of the revolution proved to be twofold: "On the one hand the arming of the people, the right of association, the sovereignty of the people actually attained; on the other hand, the preservation of the monarchy and the Camphausen-Hansemann Ministry, i.e., the government of representatives of the big bourgeoisie. Thus, the revolution had two series of results, which had inevitably to diverge. The people had achieved victory; it had won liberties of a decisive democratic nature, but the direct power passed not into its hands, but into those of the big bourgeoisie. In a word, the revolution was not completed. The people allowed the big bourgeois to form a ministry, and the big bourgeois immediately displayed their strivings by offering an alliance to the old Prussian nobility and bureaucracy. Arnim, Canitz and Schwerin joined the Ministry.

*"The upper bourgeoisie, ever antirevolutionary, concluded a defensive and offensive alliance with the reaction out of fear of the people, that is to say, the workers and the democratic bourgeoisie."*[56]  (Our italics.)

Thus, not only a "decision to organize a constituent assembly," but even its actual convocation is insufficient for a decisive victory of the revolution! Even after a partial victory in an armed struggle (the victory of the Berlin workers over the troops on March 18, 1848) an "incomplete" revolution, a revolution "that has not been carried to completion," is possible. On what, then, does its completion depend? It depends on whose hands the immediate rule passes into, whether into the hands of the Petrunkeviches and Rodichevs, that is to say, the Camphausens and the Hansemanns, or into the hands of the *people*, i.e., the workers and the democratic bourgeoisie. In the first case the bourgeoisie will possess power, and the proletariat "freedom of criticism," freedom to "remain the party of extreme revolutionary opposition." Immediately after the victory, the bourgeoisie will conclude an alliance with the reaction (this would inevitably happen in Russia too, if, for example, the St. Petersburg workers gained only a partial victory in street fighting with the troops and left it to Messrs. Petrunkeviches and Co. to form a government). In the second case, a revolutionary-democratic dictatorship, i.e., the complete victory of the revolution, would be possible.

It now remains to define more precisely what Marx really meant by "democratic bourgeoisie" (demokratische Bürgerschaft), which together with the workers he called the people, in contradistinction to the big bourgeoisie.

A clear answer to this question is supplied by the following passage from an article in the *Neue Rheinische Zeitung* of July 29, 1848: ". . . The German revolution of 1848 is only a parody of the French revolution of 1789.

"On August 4, 1789, three weeks after the storming of the Bastille, the French people in a single day prevailed over all the feudal burdens.

"On July 11, 1848, four months after the March barricades, the feudal burdens prevailed over the German people. Teste Gierke cum Hansemanno.*

---

* "Witnesses: Herr Gierke and Herr Hansemann." Hansemann was a minister who represented the party of the big bourgeoisie (Russian counterpart: Trubetskoy or Rodichev, and the like); Gierke was Minister of Agriculture in the Hansemann Cabinet, who drew up a plan, a "bold" plan for "abolishing feudal burdens," professedly "without compensation," but in fact for abolishing only the minor and unimportant burdens while preserving or granting compensation for the more essential ones. Herr Gierke was something like the Russian Messrs. Kablukov, Manuilov, Hertzenstein and similar bourgeois liberal friends of the muzhik who desire the "extension of peasant landownership" but do not wish to offend the landlords.

"The French bourgeoisie of 1789 did not for a moment leave its allies, the peasants, in the lurch. It knew that the foundation of its rule was the destruction of feudalism in the countryside, the creation of a free landowning (grundbesitzenden) peasant class.

"The German bourgeoisie of 1848 is without the least compunction betraying the peasants, who are its most natural allies, the flesh of its flesh, and without whom it is powerless against the nobility.

"The continuance of feudal rights, their sanction under the guise of (illusory) redemption — such is the result of the German revolution of 1848. The mountain brought forth a mouse."[57]

This is a very instructive passage: it gives us four important propositions: 1) The incompleted German revolution differs from the completed French revolution in that the German bourgeoisie betrayed not only democracy in general, but also the peasantry in particular. 2) The foundation for the full consummation of a democratic revolution is the creation of a free class of peasants. 3) The creation of such a class means the abolition of feudal burdens, the destruction of feudalism, but does not yet mean a socialist revolution. 4) The peasants are the "most natural" allies of the bourgeoisie, that is to say, of the democratic bourgeoisie, which without them is "powerless" against the reaction.

Making proper allowances for concrete national peculiarities and substituting serfdom for feudalism, all these propositions can be fully applied to Russia in 1905. There is no doubt that by learning from the experience of Germany, as elucidated by Marx, we cannot arrive at any other slogan for a decisive victory of the revolution than: a revolutionary-democratic dictatorship of the proletariat and the peasantry. There is no doubt that the chief components of the "people," whom Marx in 1848 contrasted with the resisting reactionaries and the treacherous bourgeoisie, are the proletariat and the peasantry. There is no doubt that in Russia too the liberal bourgeoisie and the gentlemen of the Osvobozhdeniye League are betraying and will continue to betray the peasantry, i.e., will confine themselves to a pseudo reform and taking the side of the landlords in the decisive battle between them and the peasantry. Only the proletariat is capable of supporting the peasantry to the end in this struggle. There is no doubt, finally, that in Russia also the success of the peasant struggle, i.e., the transfer of the whole of the land to the peasantry, will signify a complete democratic revolution and constitute the social support of the revolution carried to its completion, but it will by no means be a socialist revolution, or "socialization" that the ideologists of the petty bourgeoisie, the Socialist-Revolutionaries talk about. The success of the peasant insurrection, the victory of the democratic revolution will merely clear the way for a genuine and decisive struggle for Socialism on the basis of a democratic republic. In this struggle the peasantry as a landowning class will play the same treacherous, vacillating part as is now being played by the bourgeoisie in the struggle for democracy. To forget this is to forget Socialism, to deceive oneself and others as to the real interests and tasks of the proletariat.

In order to leave no gaps in the presentation of the views held by Marx in 1848, it is necessary to note one essential difference between German Social-Democracy of that time (or the Communist Party of the Proletariat, to use the language of that period) and present-day Russian Social-Democracy. Here is what Mehring says:

153

"The *Neue Rheinische Zeitung* appeared in the political arena as the 'organ of democracy.' The red thread that ran through all its articles is unmistakable. But directly, it championed the interests of the bourgeois revolution against absolutism and feudalism more than the interests of the proletariat against the bourgeoisie. Very little is to be found in its columns about the separate working-class movement during the years of the revolution, although one should not forget that along with it there appeared twice a week, under the editorship of Moll and Schapper, a special organ of the Cologne Workers' League.[58] At any rate, the present-day reader will be struck by the little attention the *Neue Rheinische Zeitung* paid to the German working-class movement of its day, although its most capable mind, Stephan Born, was a pupil of Marx and Engels in Paris and Brussels and in 1848 was the Berlin correspondent for their newspaper. Born relates in his *Memoirs* that Marx and Engels never expressed a single word in disapproval of his agitation among the workers; nevertheless, it appears probable from subsequent declarations of Engels' that they were dissatisfied, at least with the methods of this agitation. Their dissatisfaction was justified inasmuch as Born was obliged to make many concessions to the as yet totally undeveloped class consciousness of the proletariat in the greater part of Germany, concessions which do not stand the test of criticism from the viewpoint of the *Communist Manifesto*. Their dissatisfaction was unjustified inasmuch as Born managed nonetheless to maintain the agitation conducted by him on a relatively high plane. . . . Without doubt, Marx and Engels were historically and politically right in thinking that the primary interest of the working class was to push the bourgeois revolution forward as far as possible. . . . Nevertheless, a remarkable proof of how the elementary instinct of the working-class movement is able to correct the conceptions of the greatest minds is provided by the fact that in April 1849 they declared in favour of a specific workers' organization and decided to participate in the workers' congress, which was being prepared especially by the East Elbe (Eastern Prussia) proletariat."

Thus, it was only in April 1849, after the revolutionary newspaper had been appearing for almost a year (the *Neue Rheinische Zeitung* began publication on June 1, 1848) that Marx and Engels declared in favour of a special workers' organization! Until then they were merely running an "organ of democracy" unconnected by any organizational ties with an independent workers' party. This fact, monstrous and improbable as it may appear from our present-day standpoint, clearly shows us what an enormous difference there is between the German Social-Democratic Party of those days and the Russian Social-Democratic Labour Party of today. This fact shows how much less the proletarian features of the movement, the proletarian current within it, were in evidence in the German democratic revolution (because of the backwardness of Germany in 1848 both economically and politically — its disunity as a state). This should not be forgotten in judging Marx's repeated declarations during this period and somewhat later about the need for organizing an independent proletarian party. Marx arrived at this practical conclusion only as a result of the experience of the democratic revolution, almost a year later — so philistine, so petty-bourgeois was the whole atmosphere in Germany at that time. To us this conclusion is an old and solid acquisition of half a century's experience of international Social-Democracy — an acquisition with which we *began* to organize the Russian Social-Democratic Labour Party. In our case there can be no question, for instance, of revolutionary proletarian newspapers being outside the Social-Democratic Party of the proletariat, or of their appearing even for a moment simply as "organs of democracy."

But the contrast which had hardly begun to reveal itself between Marx and Stephan Born exists in our case in a form which is more developed by reason of the more powerful manifestation of the proletarian current in the democratic stream of our revolution. Speaking of the probable dissatisfaction of Marx and Engels with the agitation conducted by Stephan Born, Mehring expresses himself too mildly and too evasively. This is what Engels wrote of Born in 1885 (in his preface to the *Enthüllungen über den Kommunistenprocess zu Köln.* Zürich, 1885[59]):

The members of the Communist League[60] everywhere stood at the head of the extreme democratic movement, proving thereby that the League was an excellent school of revolutionary action. ". . . the compositor Stephan Born, who had worked in Brussels and Paris as an active member of the League, founded a Workers' Brotherhood" ("Arbeiterverbrüderung") "in Berlin which became fairly widespread and existed until 1850. Born, a very talented young man, who, however, was a bit too much in a hurry to become a big political figure, 'fraternized' with the most miscellaneous ragtag and bobtail" (Kreti und Plethi) "in order to get a crowd together, and was not at all the man who could bring unity into the conflicting tendencies, light into the chaos. Consequently, in the official publications of the association the views represented in the *Communist Manifesto* were mingled hodgepodge with guild recollections and guild as-

pirations, fragments of Louis Blanc and Proudhon, pro-
tectionism, etc.; in short, they wanted to please everybody
[*allen alles sein*]." *"In particular, strikes, trade unions and
producers' cooperatives were set going and it was forgotten
that above all it was a question of first conquering, by
means of political victories, the field* in which alone such
things could be realized on a lasting basis." (Our italics.)
"When, afterwards, the victories of the reaction made the
leaders of the Brotherhood realize the necessity of taking
a direct part in the revolutionary struggle, they were naturally left in the lurch by the confused mass which they had
grouped around themselves. Born took part in the Dresden
uprising in May, 1849 and had a lucky escape. But, in
contrast to the great political movement of the proletariat,
the Workers' Brotherhood proved to be a pure *Sonderbund*
[separate league], which to a large extent existed only on
paper and played such a subordinate role that the reaction
did not find it necessary to suppress it until 1850, and its
surviving branches until several years later. Born, whose
real name was Buttermilch" (Buttermilk),* "has not become

---

* In translating Engels I made a mistake in the first edition by taking
the word *Buttermilch* to be not a proper noun but a common noun.
This mistake naturally afforded great delight to the Mensheviks. Koltsov
wrote that I had "rendered Engels more profound" (reprinted in *Two
Years,* a collection of articles) and Plekhanov even now recalls this
mistake in the *Tovarishch*[61] — in short, it afforded *an excellent pretext
to slur over the question of the two tendencies in the working-class
movement* of 1848 in Germany, the Born tendency (akin to our Economists) and the Marxist tendency. To take advantage of the mistake of
an opponent, even if it was only on the question of Born's name, is
more than natural. But to use a correction to a translation to slur over
the question of the two tactics is to dodge the real issue. [Author's
note to the 1907 edition.]

a big political figure but a petty Swiss professor, who no longer translates Marx into guild language but the meek Renan into his own fulsome German."[62]

That is how Engels judged the two tactics of Social-Democracy in the democratic revolution!

Our new *Iskra*-ists are also pushing towards "Economism," and with such unreasonable zeal as to earn the praises of the monarchist bourgeoisie for their "seeing the light." They too collect around themselves a motley crowd, flattering the "Economists," demagogically attracting the undeveloped masses by the slogans of "initiative," "democracy," "autonomy," etc., etc. Their labour unions, too, exist only on the pages of the Khlestakov[63] new *Iskra*. Their slogans and resolutions betray a similar failure to understand the tasks of the "great political movement of the proletariat."

Written in June-July 1905

First published as a
pamphlet in Geneva
in July 1905

Published according
to the text of the pamphlet,
checked against the manuscript

# NOTES

<sup>1</sup> *Two Tactics of Social-Democracy in the Democratic Revolution* was written by Lenin in Geneva, in June-July 1905. The book was published in late July 1905, in Geneva, by the Central Committee of the R.S.D.L.P. It was twice reprinted in Russia in the same year, once by the Central Committee of the R.S.D.L.P., and the second time by the Moscow Committee of the Party, this time in 10,000 copies.

The book was secretly distributed throughout the country — in St. Petersburg, Moscow, Kazan, Tiflis, Baku and other cities. During arrests and searches the police in many cases found as many as ten or more copies of it. On February 19, 1907 it was banned by the St. Petersburg Press Department, and on December 22 of the same year the St. Petersburg Court issued an injunction for its destruction.

In 1907 Lenin had *Two Tactics* published in the miscellany *Twelve Years*, supplementing the book with new notes. The material prepared by Lenin for this book, his plans, synopsis and other notes, were published in *Lenin Miscellany*, Russ. ed., Vol. V, pp. 315-20, and Vol. XVI, pp. 151-56.

The Leninist theory of revolution and the tactical propositions which Lenin developed in his historic book *Two Tactics of Social-Democracy in the Democratic Revolution* were consistently upheld and developed by Stalin in such works as: "Armed Insurrection and Our Tactics," "The Provisional Revolutionary Government and Social-Democracy" (1905), "Two Clashes," "The Present Situation and the Unity Congress of the Workers' Party" (1906), "Preface to the Georgian Edition of K. Kautsky's Pamphlet *The Driving Forces and Prospects of the Russian Revolution*" (February 1907).

As for the historical importance of Lenin's book *Two Tactics*, see the *History of the Communist Party of the Soviet Union (Bolsheviks), Short Course*, Eng. ed., Moscow, 1950, pp. 75-93.      p. 1

[2] *Proletary (The Proletarian)* — an illegal Bolshevik weekly, the organ of the Central Committee of the R.S.D.L.P. It was founded in accordance with a resolution of the Third Congress of the Party. Lenin was appointed editor of the *Proletary* by a decision of a plenary meeting of the Party's Central Committee, on April 27 (May 10), 1905.

*Proletary* was published in Geneva from May 14 (27) to November 12 (25), 1905, a total of 26 issues being brought out. Those who took a regular part in the work of the editorial board were V. V. Vorovsky, A. V. Lunacharsky, and M. S. Olminsky. *Proletary* continued the line of the old, Leninist *Iskra*, and maintained full continuity with the Bolshevik newspaper *Vperyod*. In all, Lenin wrote over 50 articles and commentaries for *Proletary*, his articles being reprinted in local Bolshevik periodicals, and also published in the form of leaflets.

Publication of *Proletary* was discontinued in November 1905, shortly after Lenin's departure for Russia. The last two issues (Nos. 25 and 26) were edited by V. V. Vorovsky.      p. 1

[3] V. I. Lenin, *Collected Works*, 4th Russ. ed., Vol. IX, p. 127.      p. 1

[4] The mutiny broke out on June 14 (27), 1905.      p. 1

[5] *Osvobozhdeniye (Emancipation)* — a fortnightly journal of the Russian bourgeois liberals published abroad in 1902-05 under the editorship of P. B. Struve. In January 1904, it became the organ of the liberal-monarchist Osvobozhdeniye League.

Later the *Osvobozhdeniye* group formed the nucleus of the Constitutional-Democratic Party (the Cadets).      p. 4

[6] *Economism* — an opportunist trend that arose in the Russian Social-Democratic movement at the end of the 1890s. The Economists (Akimov, Martynov, and others) asserted that the task of the working class was to wage economic struggle against the employers; the political struggle against the autocracy, however, was the business of the liberal bourgeoisie, whom the working class must support. The tenets of the Economists were "a desertion of Marxism, a denial of the necessity for an independent political party of the working class, an attempt to convert the working class into a political appendage of the bourgeoisie" (*History of the Communist Party of the Soviet Union (Bolsheviks), Short Course*, Eng. ed., Moscow, 1950, p. 27). Economism was subjected to withering criticism by Lenin in his work *What Is To Be Done?* and by

Stalin in his works: "Briefly About the Disagreements in the Party," and "A Reply to *Sotsial-Demokrat*." p. 4

[7] This refers to the new, Menshevik *Iskra*. Following the Second Congress of the R.S.D.L.P., the Mensheviks gained control of the *Iskra*, with the aid of Plekhanov, and in November 1903, beginning with No. 52, *Iskra* became the organ of the Mensheviks. It continued publication until October 1905. p. 4

[8] *The Bulygin Commission* — created by a decree of the tsar in February 1905 and headed by the Minister of the Interior, A. G. Bulygin. The commission drafted a bill for the institution of a State Duma with advisory powers, and the regulations on the Duma elections. The bill and the regulations were made public together with the tsar's manifesto of August 6 (19), 1905. The Bolsheviks proclaimed an active boycott of the Bulygin Duma. The government's attempt to convene the Duma failed and it was swept away by the force of the revolution. On the boycott of the Bulygin Duma, see V. I. Lenin, *Collected Works*, 4th Russ. ed., Vol. IX, pp. 156-64. p. 7

[9] *The Constitutional-Democratic Party* (Cadets) was the principal bourgeois party in Russia, the party of the liberal-monarchist bourgeoisie. It was founded in October 1905. Under the cloak of pseudo-democratism and calling themselves the party of "people's freedom," the Cadets tried to win the peasantry to their side. They strove to preserve tsarism in the form of a constitutional monarchy. Subsequently, the Cadets became the party of the imperialist bourgeoisie. After the victory of the October Socialist Revolution, the Cadets organized counter-revolutionary conspiracies and revolts against the Soviet Republic. p. 7

[10] See V. I. Lenin, *Collected Works*, 4th Russ. ed., Vol. VIII, pp. 452-60, 477-90. p. 8

[11] *Millerandism* — an opportunist trend named after the French socialist-reformist Alexander Millerand, who in 1899 entered the reactionary bourgeois government of France, and collaborated with General Gaston Galliffet, butcher of the Paris Commune. p. 18

[12] On January 9, 1905, by order of the tsar, the troops fired at a peaceful demonstration of St. Petersburg workers who were marching towards the Winter Palace to present a petition to the tsar about their needs. This massacre touched off a wave of mass political strikes and demonstrations all over Russia. The events of January 9 marked the beginning of the first Russian revolution of 1905-07. p. 22

[13] *Die Neue Rheinische Zeitung* was published in Cologne from June 1, 1848 until May 19, 1849. It was directed by Karl Marx and Frederick Engels, Marx being editor-in-chief. Following the appearance of No. 301, the paper ceased publication because of persecution by the reactionaries. Regarding this newspaper see Engels's article "Marx and the *Neue Rheinische Zeitung* (1848-1849)" (Karl Marx and Frederick Engels, *Selected Works*, Eng. ed., Moscow, 1951, Vol. II, pp. 297-305).     p. 23

[14] *Sotsial-Demokrat (The Social-Democrat)* — a Menshevik Georgian-language newspaper published in Tiflis between April and November 1905.

The article "The Zemsky Sobor and Our Tactics" was written by N. Jordania, leader of the Caucasian Mensheviks. It was criticized in detail by Lenin in Chapter Seven of *Two Tactics of Social-Democracy in the Democratic Revolution* (see pp. 59-64 of this book).     p. 26

[15] *A constitution "à la Shipov"* — Lenin here refers to the "constitutional" platform of D. N. Shipov, one of the leaders of the Zemstvo-liberal movement of the 1890s and 1900s. The platform provided for the preservation of the tsarist autocracy slightly restricted by a "constitution" to be "granted by the tsar."     p. 28

[16] From the perspective of eternity.     p. 34

[17] The remote past.     p. 34

[18] *Russkaya Starina (The Russian Antiquary)* — a monthly journal of history published in St. Petersburg from 1870 to 1918.     p. 35

[19] See Karl Marx and Frederick Engels, *Selected Works*, Eng. ed., Moscow, 1951, Vol. II, p. 367.     p. 36

[20] *The Zemstvo* — local government bodies in pre-revolutionary Russia. They dealt with purely local affairs concerning the rural population (laying roads, building hospitals, etc.). The predominant role in the Zemstvo was played by the landlords.     p. 47

[21] *The man in the muffler* — chief character in Chekhov's story of the same title, a man typifying the narrow-minded philistine who abhors all innovations or initiative.     p. 48

[22] Lenin is referring to the book *Aus dem literarischen Nachlass von Karl Marx, Friedrich Engels und Ferdinand Lassalle, Herausgegeben von Franz Mehring*, Band III, Stuttgart, 1902, S. 211 (*Posthumous Works of Karl Marx, Frederick Engels, Ferdinand Lassalle edited by Franz Mehring*, Vol. III, Stuttgart, 1902, p. 211). See Karl Marx, "The Bourgeoisie and the Counter-revolution" (Karl Marx and Frederick Engels, *Selected Works*, Eng. ed., Moscow, 1951, Vol. I, p. 63).     p. 55

[23] Lenin here refers to his article " 'Revolutionaries' in White Gloves," published in *Proletary*, No. 5, 1905 (*Collected Works*, 4th Russ. ed., Vol. VIII, pp. 491-95). p. 56

[24] *Vperyodovtsi, Syezdovtsi, Proletartsi* — different appellations for the Bolsheviks arising from the fact that they published the newspaper *Vperyod*, that they convened the Third Congress of the Party, and from the name of the newspaper *Proletary*. p. 56

[25] This refers to the resolution tabled by Starover (pseudonym of the Menshevik A. N. Potresov) on the attitude towards the liberals, which was adopted at the Second Congress of the R.S.D.L.P., and was criticized by Lenin in the article "Working-class and Bourgeois Democracy" (*Collected Works*, 4th Russ. ed., Vol. VIII, pp. 54-63). p. 57

[26] The expression "parliamentary cretinism" was applied by Lenin to those opportunists who considered the parliamentarian system all-powerful, and parliamentarian activities the only or the principal form of political struggle. p. 62

[27] This refers to the differences of opinion revealed during the discussion of the draft agrarian programme at the Breslau Congress of the German Social-Democratic Party, 1895. p. 64

[28] *Rabocheye Dyelo (The Workers' Cause)* — a journal of the Economists published irregularly in Geneva from 1899 to 1902 as the organ of the Union of Russian Social-Democrats Abroad. For a criticism of the *Rabocheye Dyelo* group, see Lenin's *What Is To Be Done?* (*Selected Works*, Eng. ed., Moscow, 1950, Vol. I, Part 1, pp. 203-409). p. 71

[29] This refers to Nadezhdin's press attack on the plan of the Leninist *Iskra* (Nadezhdin was the pseudonym of Y. O. Zelensky). Lenin criticized this attack as far back as 1902 in his *What Is To Be Done?* p. 71

[30] *Bernsteinism* — an anti-Marxist trend in international Social-Democracy. It arose towards the close of the 19th century and took its name from the German Social-Democrat Eduard Bernstein, who tried to revise the revolutionary teachings of Marx on the lines of bourgeois liberalism. In Russia this trend was represented by the "Legal Marxists," the Economists, the Bundists, and the Mensheviks. p. 78

[31] This refers to Lenin's articles entitled "Social-Democracy and the Provisional Revolutionary Government" and "The Revolutionary Democratic Dictatorship of the Proletariat and the Peasantry," which were published in Nos. 13 and 14 of the Bolshevik newspaper *Vperyod* (*Collected Works*, 4th Russ. ed., Vol. VIII, pp. 247-74). p. 81

[32] Lenin has in view the programme published in 1874 by the London group of Blanquists, former members of the Paris Commune. See Frederick Engels, "Emigré Literature. II. The Programme of the Blanquist Emigrés from the Commune" (Karl Marx and Frederick Engels, *Collected Works*, Ger. ed., 1935, Vol. XV, pp. 224-30).

The *Blanquists* were adherents of the French revolutionary Louis Auguste Blanqui (1805-81). The classics of Marxism-Leninism, while regarding Blanqui as an outstanding revolutionary and adherent of socialism, criticized him for his sectarianism and conspiratorial methods of activity.

"Blanquism," wrote Lenin, "is a theory that repudiates the class struggle. Blanquism expects that mankind will be emancipated from wage slavery, not by the class struggle of the proletariat, but through a conspiracy hatched by a small minority of intellectuals" (see V. I. Lenin, "The Congress Summed Up", *Collected Works*, 4th Russ. ed., Vol. X, p. 360).                                                                                                                                            p. 84

[33] *The Erfurt Programme* of German Social-Democracy was adopted in October 1891 at a congress held in Erfurt. For a criticism of this programme, see Frederick Engels, "Criticism of the Draft Social-Democratic Programme of 1891" (Karl Marx and Frederick Engels, *Collected Works*, Russ. ed., 1936, Vol. XVI, pp. 101-16), and Lenin's *The State and Revolution*.                                                                                                                     p. 91

[34] In July 1905 Lenin wrote this note to Chapter Ten of *Two Tactics of Social-Democracy in the Democratic Revolution*. The note did not go into the first edition of the book, and first appeared in 1926, in *Lenin Miscellany*, Russ. ed., Vol. V.                                                           p. 92

[35] See Karl Marx and Frederick Engels, *Selected Correspondence*, Moscow, 1953, pp. 551-55.                                                             p. 92

[36] Lenin here refers to his article "Social-Democracy and the Provisional Revolutionary Government," published in *Vperyod*, No. 14, 1905 (*Collected Works*, 4th Russ. ed., Vol. VIII, pp. 247-63).                        p. 92

[37] Lenin has in view his article "On the Provisional Revolutionary Government" (*Collected Works*, 4th Russ. ed., Vol. VIII, pp. 427-47), and also the article by Frederick Engels, "The Bakuninists at Work. Notes on the Insurrection in Spain in the Summer of 1873," in which the Bakuninist resolution referred to by Lenin is criticized (see Karl Marx and Frederick Engels, *Collected Works*, Russ. ed., 1935, Vol. XV, pp. 105-24).                                                                                             p. 101

[38] *Credo* was the name by which became known the manifesto issued in 1899 by a group of Economists including S. N. Prokopovich and

E. D. Kuskova who later became Constitutional-Democrats. This manifesto was a most striking expression of the opportunism of Russian Economism. Lenin wrote a trenchant protest denouncing the Economists' views ("A Protest of Russian Social-Democrats," *Collected Works*, 4th Russ. ed., Vol. IV, pp. 149-63). p. 103

[39] *Rabochaya Mysl (Workers' Thought)* — organ of the Economists, published in 1897-1902. Lenin criticized the views of this newspaper as a Russian variety of international opportunism in a number of his works, particularly in his articles in *Iskra* and in his book *What Is To Be Done?*
p. 104

[40] This refers to Marx's words in his "A Contribution to the Critique of Hegel's Philosophy of Law" (Karl Marx and Frederick Engels, *Collected Works*, Ger. ed., Berlin, 1956, Vol. I, p. 385). p. 104

[41] *L'Humanité* — a daily paper founded in 1904 by Jean Jaurès as the organ of the French Socialist Party. Soon after the split in the Socialist Party at the Tours Congress (December 1920) and the formation of the Communist Party of France, the paper became the organ of the latter. It is still published in Paris at present as the official organ of the C.P.F. p. 106

[42] *Varlin, Louis-Eugène* (1839-71) — French worker and prominent member of the First International, member of the Central Committee of the National Guard and of the Paris Commune of 1871. p. 118

[43] This refers to the "Rules of Organization" adopted at the Geneva Menshevik Conference in 1905. The "Rules" were also criticized by Lenin in the article "A Third Step Back" (*Collected Works*, 4th Russ. ed., Vol. VIII, pp. 509-18) and in "Preface to the Pamphlet *Workers on the Split in the Party*" (*ibid.*, Vol. IX, pp. 141-46). p. 120

[44] See Karl Marx, "The Class Struggles in France, 1848 to 1850" (Karl Marx and Frederick Engels, *Selected Works*, Moscow, 1951, Vol. I, p. 198). p. 124

[45] *The Hirsch-Duncker trade unions* — founded in 1868 in Germany by two bourgeois liberals — Hirsch and Duncker who, like the bourgeois economist Brentano, preached "harmony of class interests," distracted the workers from the revolutionary class struggle against the bourgeoisie, and limited the role of the trade unions to the bounds of mutual-aid societies and educational clubs. p. 132

[46] Engels's article "The Bakuninists at Work. Notes on the Insurrection in Spain in the Summer of 1873" was translated into Russian under

Lenin's editorship and was published in 1905 in Geneva by the Central Committee of the R.S.D.L.P. in the form of a pamphlet. A second edition came out in 1906 in St. Petersburg.

The *Address of the Central Committee to the Communist League* (March 1850) was published in Russian in 1906 in the supplement to Marx's pamphlet *Revelations About the Trial of the Communists at Cologne*, which was brought out by the *Molot* Publishers in St. Petersburg (see Karl Marx and Frederick Engels, *Selected Works*, Eng. ed., Moscow, 1951, Vol. I, pp. 98-108).                                                    p. 136

[47] V. I. Lenin, *Collected Works*, 4th Russ. ed., Vol. V, pp. 19-65.

p. 139

[48] From the beginning of this paragraph to ". . . at the tail of *Osvobozhdeniye*-ism?" on p. 144 was omitted in the first edition of this book. This passage was first published in *Pravda*, No. 112, April 22, 1940.                                                                           p. 142

[49] Karl Marx and Frederick Engels, *Selected Works*, Eng. ed., Moscow, 1951, Vol. I, pp. 429-94.                                             p. 142

[50] *Moskovskiye Vyedomosti (Moscow Recorder)* — a newspaper founded in 1756. From the 1860s it expressed the views of the most reactionary monarchist sections of the landlords and the clergy. In 1905 it became a leading organ of the Black Hundreds, and was banned following the October Revolution of 1917.                                                p. 143

[51] *Mehring, Franz* (1846-1919) — a prominent member of the Left-wing of German Social-Democracy, historian and publicist. He was one of the founders of the revolutionary Spartacus League, and later joined the Communist Party of Germany.                                          p. 146

[52] See Karl Marx and Frederick Engels, *Collected Works*, Ger. ed., Berlin, 1959, Vol. V, p. 402.                                             p. 147

[53] *Ibid.*, p. 40.                                                       p. 148

[54] *Ibid.*, p. 41.                                                       p. 149

[55] *Ibid.*, p. 14.                                                       p. 149

[56] *Ibid.*, pp. 64-65.                                                   p. 150

[57] *Ibid.*, pp. 382-83.                                                  p. 152

[58] The organ of the Cologne Workers' League was originally called *Zeitung des Arbeiter-Vereins zu Köln*, with the subtitle *Freiheit, Brüderlichkeit, Arbeit (Freedom, Brotherhood, Labour)*. Its editors, Joseph Moll and Karl Schapper, were members of the Communist League. Forty issues came out between April and October 1848, and another 23 between

October 1848 and June 1849, during which period the subtitle became the paper's title. p. 154

[59] *Revelations About the Trial of the Communists at Cologne*, Zurich, 1885. p. 156

[60] *The Communist League* — the first international organization of the revolutionary proletariat founded in London in the summer of 1847 at a congress of delegates from revolutionary proletarian organizations. The League was organized and guided by Karl Marx and Frederick Engels, who, on instructions from the League, wrote its programme — the *Manifesto of the Communist Party*. The League existed until 1852. Later its foremost members played a leading part in the First International. See Frederick Engels's article "On the History of the Communist League" (Karl Marx and Frederick Engels, *Selected Works*, Eng. ed., Moscow, 1951, Vol. II, pp. 306-23). p. 156

[61] *Tovarishch (The Comrade)* — a daily newspaper published in St. Petersburg from March 1906 till January 1908. Though formally not the organ of any particular party, it was in fact the mouthpiece of the Left Constitutional-Democrats. Mensheviks also contributed to the paper. p. 157

[62] See Karl Marx and Frederick Engels, *Selected Works*, Eng. ed., Moscow, 1951, Vol. II, pp. 318-19. p. 158

[63] *Khlestakov* — the leading character in Gogol's comedy *The Inspector-General*, an arrant boaster and liar. p. 158